sew modern baby

19 Projects to Sew from Cuddly Sleepers to Stimulating Toys

Angela Yosten

Text and Photography copyright © 2013 by Angela Yosten

Photography and Artwork copyright © 2013 by C&T Publishing, Inc.

PUBLISHER: Amy Marson

CREATIVE DIRECTOR: Gailen Runge

ART DIRECTOR: Kristy Zacharias

EDITORS: S. Michele Fry and Jill Mordick

TECHNICAL EDITORS: Sandy Peterson,
Susan Hendrickson, and Teresa Stroin

COVER DESIGNERS: Christina Jarumay Fox
and Kristy Zacharias

BOOK DESIGNER: Christina Jarumay Fox

PRODUCTION COORDINATORS: Jessica Jenkins
and Jenny Davis

PRODUCTION EDITORS: Joanna Burgarino
and Katie Van Amburg

ILLUSTRATOR: Jessica Jenkins

PHOTO ASSISTANT: Mary Peyton Peppo

Style Photography by Christina Carty-
Francis; How-To Photography by
Angela Yosten; Photography by Diane
Pedersen of C&T Publishing, Inc., unless
otherwise noted

Published by Stash Books, an imprint of C&T Publishing, Inc., P.O. Box 1456,
Lafayette, CA 94549

Library of Congress Cataloging-in-Publication Data

Yosten, Angela, 1980-

 Sew modern baby : 19 projects to sew from cuddly sleepers to stimulating toys
/ Angela Yosten.

   pages cm

 ISBN 978-1-60705-735-2 (soft cover)

1. Infants' clothing. 2. Infants' supplies. 3. Soft toy making. 4. Sewing. I. Title. II.
Title: Sew Modern baby.

 TT637.Y67 2013

 745.592'4--dc23

                    2013000948

Printed in China

10 9 8 7 6 5 4 3 2 1

acknowledgments

This book is dedicated to my children, Paige, Matthew, and Roman. I love each and every one of you in your own special ways. Thank you for being the best children a mother could ever have and for always being there when I need a hug. I love you, really!

Thank you to my hubby, Richie, for being the best lifelong partner and daddy to our children a girl could dream of. I love you very much and could not have written this book without your continued support and encouragement.

Thank you to my mom, Karen, for always being just a call away and dropping everything at a moment's notice to help me when I need you. Whether it is just to chat, be granny, or help me with projects, I truly appreciate it. Love you lots!

Thank you to my mother-in-law, Darlene. I will always be grateful to you for bringing your son into my life and caring so deeply for our family. Hugs!

Thank you to Gailen Runge, Liz Aneloski, and everyone else at C&T Publishing / Stash Books who was able to see my vision and support me through the publishing process. I said it once, and I'll say it again—you all ROCK!

contents

introduction

The arrival of a new baby brings about so many new emotions and experiences. A mother and child develop a bond like no other. No matter how many kids you have, whether one or twenty, each mother-child relationship is unique.

Vision is one of the most important senses we use in learning, but it is one of the slowest senses to develop. When an infant is born, the number of colors and shapes he or she can see is limited. Researchers believe that after black and white, red is the first color a baby can see. That is followed by orange, yellow, green, and finally blue.

The projects presented in this book were designed with exactly this in mind. I strategically used high-contrast colors and simple shapes to help with brain stimulation and the development of a newborn. But I also used natural linen elements to create an heirloom quality to the projects, so they can be passed down through generations. Other fun developmental tools used in the projects include squeakers and rattles for developing the sense of hearing.

I don't know if it was age or having our third child that made me realize the importance of educating children at an early age and providing them with creative ways to learn. In this book you will find 19 fun and inspirational projects that both baby and mom can enjoy.

some basic information

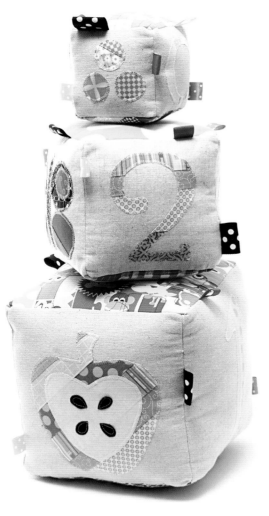

TOOLS AND SUPPLIES

I will refer to some of the tools listed below throughout the book. Check back here as often as you like to help get a better understanding of what you are working with.

CLOSURES—Buttons, grommets, hooks, snaps, and zippers are just a few of the closures that are used in the projects presented in this book. It is always fun to experiment with new ways to use traditional types of closures in your projects.

FABRICS—Using quality fabrics is key to having a long-lasting quilt or project that you can cherish for many years.

FILLERS—Pillow forms, quilt batting, and stuffing are the most commonly used fillers in the industry. Typically, these items are made of a cotton/polyester blend. However, new technologies have made natural fibers such as soy, bamboo, and natural cotton more easily available and widely used. Pillow forms make stuffing a pillow fast and easy without all the mess of loose fiberfill stuffing. Quilt batting is a thin, soft layer that is placed between a quilt top and backing to create warmth and comfort.

FUSIBLE WEB—A staple in appliqué, this paper-backed double-sided adhesive makes sewing appliqué, both large and small, a breeze. Activated by the heat of an iron, the adhesive helps keep the appliqué fused to the project while you are stitching around the raw edges to keep the design in place for years to come. Follow the manufacturer's instructions when pressing.

INTERFACING—Interfacings help add weight and stability to fabrics where needed. They come in various weights and thicknesses to work in any project.

MEASURING TAPE—An extra-long flexible measuring tape will come in handy for the larger projects in this book.

NEEDLES—You will still need a sewing needle to hand stitch openings closed on some of the projects. Any size hand needle will do.

POINT TURNER—Having a good point turner can really make a difference when turning sharp corners on a project. Point turners are made specifically to help push out the corners on a bag, pillow, or other project when turning the piece right side out. Try not to use scissors to push out the corners, as this could damage your project.

ROTARY CUTTER—Rotary cutters come in a few sizes; the most commonly used is a 45mm rotary cutter. Be sure to always have a sharp blade to help maintain perfect cutting every time.

ROTARY CUTTING MAT—A self-healing rotary mat with gridlines is used in conjunction with the rotary cutter and ruler. These tools will help make your cutting go much quicker.

ROTARY RULER—I personally like to use an 8½″ × 24″ ruler; however, a ruler any width × 24″ will work great.

SCISSORS—Sharp pairs of fabric scissors, both long and short, are essential for cutting out all the curves and corners on your appliqué. Never use your fabric scissors on paper.

SEAM RIPPER—Everyone makes mistakes once in a while, so be sure to have a seam ripper on hand for those unwanted oopsies. I use a seam ripper with a retractable blade.

SPRAY STARCH—Using a good spray starch will help you press out the wrinkles and folds in fabrics.

STRAIGHT PINS—Straight pins are very useful for holding fabrics together while machine sewing. But be sure to pull those pins out before you get to them; don't sew over them because they may break your machine needle.

TEMPLATE PATTERNS—Full-size patterns for each project are supplied in this book and on the pullout page. *The patterns are reversed for fusible appliqué.* I recommend tracing the patterns on tracing paper or paper-backed fusible web to maintain the original patterns for multiple uses.

THREAD—Several kinds of threads are available in the quilting and sewing industry. A good-quality thread, such as Aurifil, will last a lifetime and will not split or break while sewing. I use two different weights in this book, 12-weight for embroidery and 50-weight for project construction.

CREATING A BASE FOR SCRAP APPLIQUÉ

What is a scrap appliqué? Many would define it as a small piece of scrap fabric cut into a shape and either hand or machine sewn to another piece of fabric or article of clothing. For a modern look, I take it a step further by stitching several pieces of fabric together to create a scrappier style of appliqué.

1. Dump all your scraps on the floor and sort them by color. I have already sorted my scraps by color and put each colorway into clear zippered storage bags. You can also create scraps by cutting various sizes of strips from yardage.

2. Sew similarly colored scraps together in strips to create a fabric base. (This is called strip piecing.)

3. Press the seam allowances in the same direction; top-stitching the seams is optional.

4. Use this fabric base for your scrap appliqué shapes or as background fabric.

BINDING

Binding is an essential last step in making a quilt. It is what completes the project and gives your quilt a clean, finished look. Binding holds it all together so that the quilt can be cherished for years to come.

1. Cut 2½″ binding strips as directed in the instructions for each pattern.

2. Lay 2 strips end to end at a 90° angle, with right sides together. Draw a diagonal line from corner to corner and stitch on that line. Trim to a ¼″ seam allowance and press the seams open. Continue until all the strips are sewn together. (Figure A)

3. Cut the beginning end of the joined binding strip at a 45° angle. Fold the trimmed end under ¼″ and press. Trim the overhanging "bunny's ear." (Figure B)

4. Fold the long strip in half lengthwise, with wrong sides together, and press. (Figure C)

5. On the right side of the quilt, starting on the top edge, match up the raw edges of the binding to the raw edges of the quilt. Backstitch and sew with a ⅜″ seam allowance, starting about 4″–6″ from the beginning (trimmed end) of the binding.

6. Stitch along the top of the quilt. When you reach ⅜″ from the corner of the quilt, backstitch and remove the quilt from the machine. (Figure D)

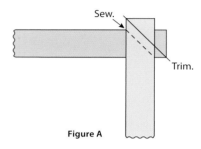

Sew.
Trim.

Figure A

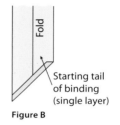

Fold

Starting tail of binding (single layer)

Figure B

Figure C

End stitching ⅜″ from corner.

Figure D

7. Fold the tail of the binding up so it forms a 45° angle and then back down, aligning the binding raw edge with the raw edge of the quilt. Press. (Figures E and F)

8. Begin stitching again from the corner, with a ⅜″ seam allowance.

9. Continue to stitch and fold at each corner until you come back to where you started. Stop and backstitch about 4″ from the beginning tail end. Remove the quilt from the machine.

10. Overlap the beginning and ending tails and trim the ending tail at 90°, keeping a 2″ overlap.

11. Insert the ending tail into the "pocket" of the folded beginning tail. (Figure G)

12. Stitch the remaining section of binding to the quilt, sewing slightly beyond the starting stitches.

13. Fold the binding to the quilt back and hand stitch, mitering the corners.

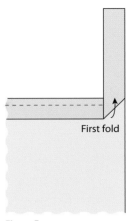

First fold

Figure E

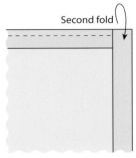

Second fold

Figure F

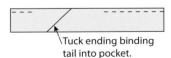

Tuck ending binding tail into pocket.

Figure G

From infants to toddlers, this play gym will help keep your child busy learning colors and numbers. The ribbon loops allow you to add fun toys that baby can look at and play with.

1 play gym

Quilted by Natalia Bonner **Finished gym:** *36½″ × 36½″*

MATERIALS

WOF = width of fabric

Play mat

- 1 yard of linen fabric

- 9 different colored fabric scraps, each measuring 8″ × 8″ (½ yard total)

- ⅝ yard *or* 8 strip-bundle strips (2½″ × WOF) of white solid fabric

- 1⅜ yards of coordinating fabric for the backing (44″–45″ wide)

- ½ yard of coordinating fabric for the binding

- 45″ × 45″ quilt batting

- 1 yard of fusible web

Arches

- 10′ of ½″ flexible blue plastic conduit tubing (corrugated)

- 2 pieces 6′ long of 2″-diameter pre-slit pipe insulation that fits the ½″ tubing

- 14 fat eighths (9″ × 22″) for the tubes

- 10″ × 10″ square of fabric

- 10″ × 10″ square of fusible interfacing (Shape-Flex by C&T Publishing)

- 4½″ piece of ¾″-wide hook-and-loop tape

- Pipe cutter or sharp box knife

Other materials

- 12″ piece of 1½″-wide grosgrain ribbon

- 20″ piece of ⅞″-wide grosgrain ribbon

- 12″ piece of ⅝″-wide grosgrain ribbon

- Coordinating thread, 12-weight for embroidery (*optional*) and 50-weight for project construction

- 8 baby play rings (approximately 2″ × 2½″ ovals with openings)

play mat

From the linen fabric:
- 9 squares 10″ × 10″

From the white fabric:
- 6 strips 2½″ × 10″
- 4 strips 2½″ × 33″
- 2 strips 2½″ × 37″

From the ⅝″-wide grosgrain ribbon:
- 4 pieces, each 2″ long

APPLIQUÉ

Template patterns are on pages 23–27.

1. If you are using scraps for the appliqué, sew the scraps together first to create a base fabric piece 8″ × 8″ for each of the 9 numbers. Press all the seams in one direction.

2. Trace the number appliqué template patterns on the paper side of the fusible web. Loosely cut around each of the traced shapes.

> ❈ note
>
> *The number templates are already reversed for you, so simply trace and fuse.*

3. Position the adhesive side of the fusible web to the wrong side of your chosen fabric for the appropriate number template. Press. Cut along the traced lines.

4. Remove the paper backing and center the number on a linen fabric square. Press in place.

5. Repeat this process until all 9 numbers are fused onto the linen fabric squares.

6. Machine appliqué around each number using your favorite stitch type. I chose a small buttonhole stitch.

PIECING

All seams are ¼″ unless otherwise noted.

1. Fold each of the 4 ribbon pieces in half crosswise, matching the raw edges, and stitch with a ⅛″ seam to hold the ends in place. Set aside.

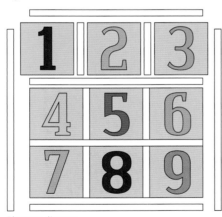

2. Using the diagram as a guide, stitch the 2½″ × 10″ strips between the number blocks, working from left to right to create 3 rows of numbers.

Play mat diagram

3. Moving from top to bottom, stitch the 2½″ × 33″ strips above the first row, between the rows of numbers, and below the bottom row.

4. Aligning the raw edges, pin and, using a ⅛″ seam allowance, stitch the folded ribbon pieces from Step 1 in the following locations:

   - Left center on block 1
   - Left center on block 7
   - Right center on block 3
   - Right center on block 9

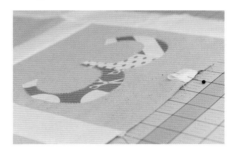

5. Finally, stitch the 2½″ × 37″ strips to the left and right sides of the play mat.

6. *Optional:* Using a 12-weight thread, hand stitch around each number block in the white sashing. I used a coordinating thread color for each number so it contrasted with the white background.

FINISHING

1. The batting and backing fabric should be approximately 4″ larger than the quilt top on all 4 sides. Sandwich the quilt top, batting, and backing. Quilt as desired. I have my quilt tops quilted by a professional longarm quilter.

tip

When quilting, be sure the ribbon loops do not get stitched down to the quilt. These loops will hold baby rings for the arches or toys once completed.

2. Use a rotary cutter, mat, and ruler to trim excess fabric from all 4 sides of the quilt and square up the corners.

3. Cut 5 strips 2½″ × width of fabric from the binding fabric. Trim off the selvages.

4. Finish your quilt by joining the binding strips together and adding the binding to the quilt. Refer to Binding (page 12) for step-by-step instructions.

arches

1. Cut 2 pieces 5″ × 6″ from each of the 14 fat eighths (28 pieces total).

2. Mixing up the fabrics, stitch 14 pieces together along the 6″ sides. Press the seams in one direction.

3. Cut 4 pieces 3″ long from the ⅝″-, ⅞″-, and 1½″-wide ribbon. Set aside the 1½″-wide ribbon.

4. Fold the ⅝″-wide and ⅞″-wide pieces in half crosswise, matching the raw edges. Pin the ribbon pieces in place as follows:

- ⅝″-wide ribbons – place 10″ from both short sides of the strip of pieced fabric

- ⅞″-wide ribbons – place 20½″ from both short sides of the strip of pieced fabric

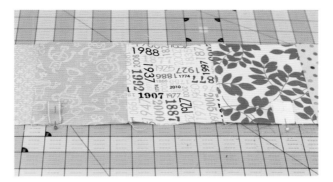

5. With right sides together, fold the long strip of fabric in half lengthwise, matching the raw edges and sandwiching the ribbon in place. Pin and stitch the long edge only, securing the ribbon. Be sure to backstitch at both ends of the tube.

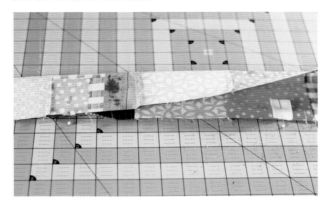

6. Turn the fabric tube right side out. Set aside.

7. Repeat Steps 2–6 for the remaining 14 pieces of fabric cut at 5″ × 6″ and the ribbon pieces.

8. Measure and cut the 2 pieces of insulation tubing to 58½″ each, using regular scissors.

9. Measure and cut 2 pieces of blue plastic conduit tubing to 58½˝ each, using a pipe cutter or box knife.

10. Carefully slip the foam insulation tubing into the fabric sleeve until the foam tubing is centered inside the fabric.

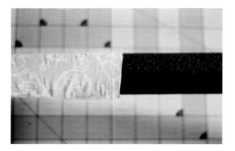

> **tip**
>
> When slipping the foam tube into the fabric sleeve, push the foam tube in the direction of the pressed seams.

11. Push the conduit tubing inside the foam tubing for additional stability.

12. Fold in the raw edges on either side of the fabric sleeve approximately 1˝.

13. Slip the raw edge of one of the folded 1½˝-wide ribbons into the end of the fabric tube and pin.

14. Stitch in place with a ⅛˝ seam. Repeat for all 4 ends.

CENTER STRAP

1. Press the 10˝ × 10˝ piece of fusible interfacing to the wrong side of the 10˝ × 10˝ piece of fabric.

2. Fold the square in half with right sides together, matching the raw edges.

3. Stitch a ¼˝ seam around the 3 raw edges, leaving a 3˝ opening for turning on the long edge. Turn the strap right side out and press.

4. Topstitch ⅛˝ from the edges around all 4 sides of the strap, closing the opening.

5. Stitch the 4½˝ hook-and-loop tape component pieces on either side of the strap. The hook-and-loop tape pieces should be on opposite sides and opposite edges.

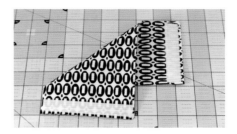

6. Place the arches side by side and wrap the strap around the center of the 2 tubes.

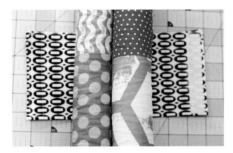

7. Attach the baby play rings to the ribbon loops at the ends of each arch and to the loops on the arches for toys. Then attach the rings of the arches onto the ribbon loops on the play mat to create a fun play gym for infants. When the child grows bigger, the arches can easily be removed so you can use just the mat for playing, learning, or tummy time.

Play Mat
Number 1
Trace 1.

Play Mat
Number 2
Trace 1.

Play Mat
Number 4
Trace 1.

Play Mat
Number 3
Trace 1.

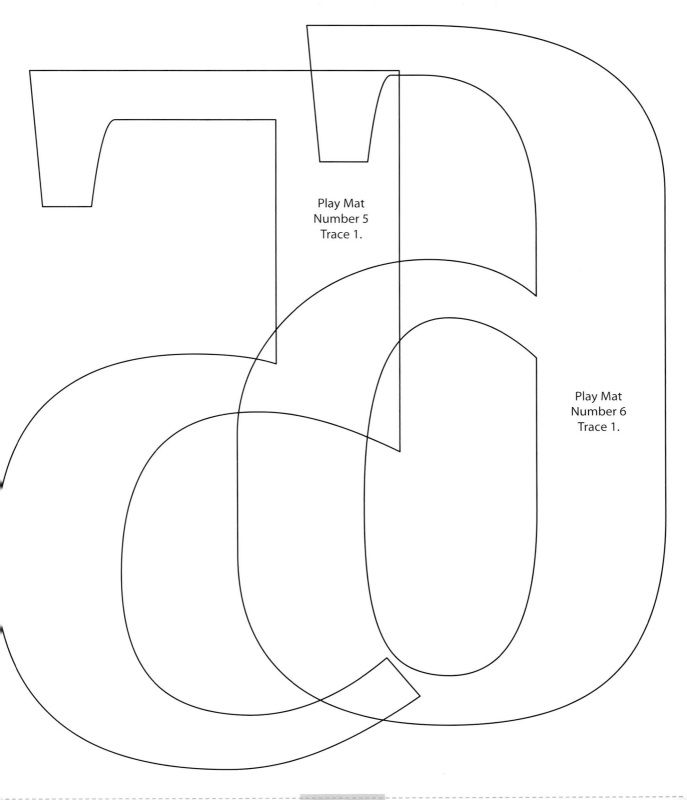

Play Mat
Number 5
Trace 1.

Play Mat
Number 6
Trace 1.

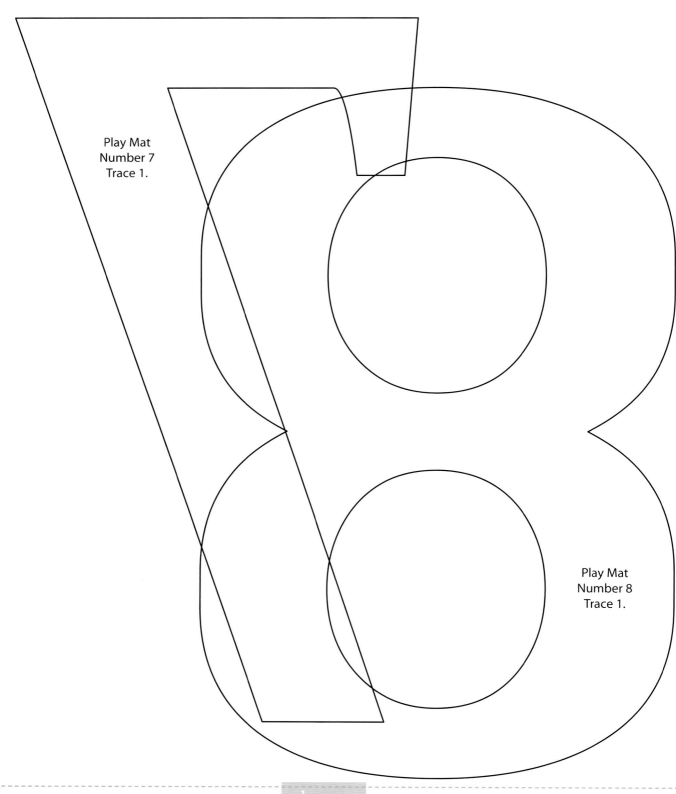

Play Mat
Number 7
Trace 1.

Play Mat
Number 8
Trace 1.

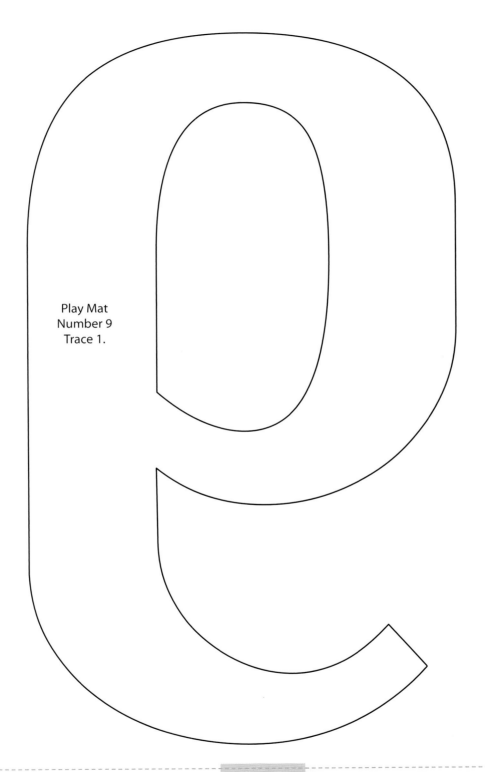

Play Mat
Number 9
Trace 1.

Hang these four little friends by their tails on the Play Gym or play with them one on one. They rattle, squeak, and make crinkle noises when certain parts of their bodies are loved.

2 animal rattles

Finished rattle: *approximately 6″ tall*

MATERIALS

(For 1 each of all 4 animal rattles)

- ½ yard of linen fabric for the animal bodies

- Miscellaneous fabric scraps the size of each animal template, measuring no larger than 6″ × 6″ each

- ½ yard of fusible web

- Polyester fiberfill

- 2 small rattles

- 2 small squeakers

- 12″ × 12″ square of crinkle material (often called crinkle paper or baby paper)

- 18″ piece of ⅝″- to ⅞″-wide grosgrain ribbon, cut into 6 pieces, each 3″ long

- Coordinating thread, 12-weight for embroidery and 50-weight for project construction

- Point turner (*optional*)

body templates and appliqué

Appliqué template patterns are on page 39 and main body part template patterns are on pullout page P1. Make and attach the appliqué pieces to the corresponding body part before joining the body parts together.

1. Follow the tracing and cutting instructions on each animal body part pattern. Cut out the main body parts.

2. If you are using scraps for an appliqué, sew all the scraps together first to create a base fabric piece about 6″ × 6″. Press all the seams in one direction.

3. Trace the appliqué templates on the paper side of the fusible web. Loosely cut around each of the traced shapes.

4. Position and press the adhesive side of the fusible web to the wrong side of your chosen appliqué fabric for the appropriate animal template. Cut along the traced lines.

5. Remove the paper backing and position the pieces on each animal body part as shown in the diagrams. Press in place. (Figures A, B, C, and D)

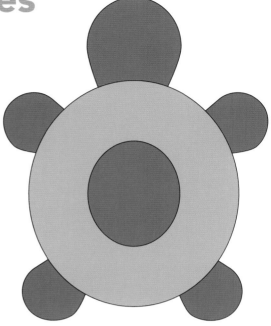

Turtle, Figure A

Panda, Figure B

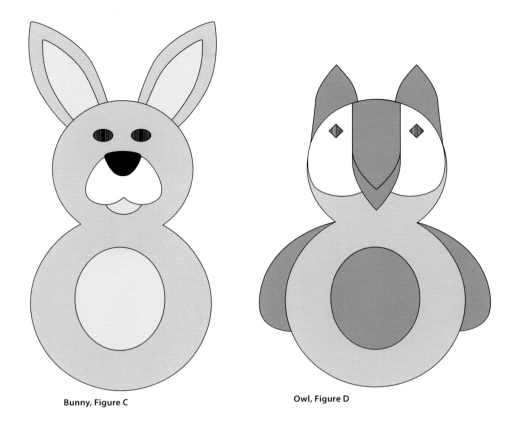

Bunny, Figure C

Owl, Figure D

6. Machine appliqué around each piece using your favorite stitch type. I chose a zigzag stitch.

tip

When cutting fabric pieces that have a front and back, match the fabric right sides together, pin the template on one side, and then cut. This will ensure that the front and back pieces line up properly when you sew them together.

turtle

All seams are ¼˝ unless otherwise noted. Trace and cut out the turtle templates. Refer to Body Templates and Appliqué and the turtle diagram (page 30) for making the body parts.

1. Place the 2 head pieces right sides together and stitch around the curved part of the head, leaving the straight end open for stuffing. Turn right side out.

2. Using just a pinch of fiberfill, stuff the head and insert a small squeaker so the stuffing wraps nicely between the squeaker and the fabric. Close the opening using a ⅛˝ seam.

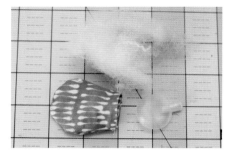

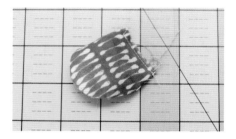

3. Lay the shell side of the turtle body faceup. Pin the head of the turtle, with raw edges together, at one end of the body. Pin the ribbon tail, folded in half with raw edges together, at the opposite end of the body. Set aside.

4. Place the leg fabrics right sides together in 4 sets of 2. Place a piece of crinkle material on top of each set.

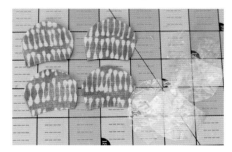

5. Stitch around the curved edge of each set, leaving the straight side open for turning. Turn right side out.

 tip

Use a point turner to help push out the small corners.

6. Pin the 4 legs on the right side of the turtle body, with raw edges together. Place the turtle belly piece right side down, covering all the little pieces tucked inside. Pin in place.

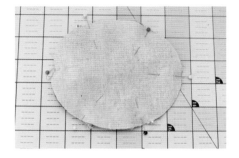

7. Starting at the head of the turtle, lift the top belly piece out of the way and stitch to attach the head to the shell piece of the body. Leave this section open for turning and stuffing.

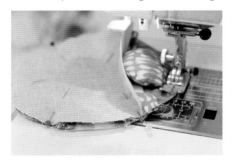

8. Stitch around the body, joining the shell and belly, leaving a 2″–3″ opening just at the head. Turn the turtle right side out.

9. Pull the head out, stuff the body, and whipstitch the opening closed.

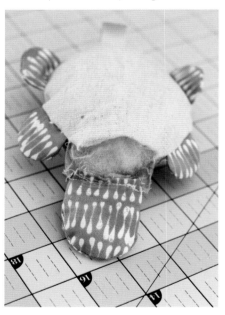

panda

All seams are ¼″ unless otherwise noted. Trace and cut out the panda templates. Refer to Body Templates and Appliqué and the panda diagram (page 30) for making the body parts.

1. On the panda body front, stitch on the nose according to the pattern instructions, using a satin stitch.

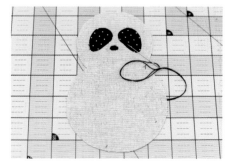

2. Place the leg and ear fabrics right sides together in sets of 2. Place a piece of crinkle material on top of each set of legs and ears.

3. Stitch around the curved edge of each set, leaving the straight side open for turning. Turn right side out.

4. Pin the legs, ears, and ribbon tail in place, with raw edges together, on the right side of the panda back.

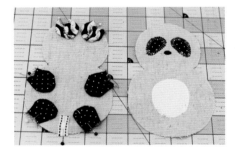

5. Place the panda front piece right side down, against the panda back, covering all the little pieces tucked inside. Pin in place. (Figure A)

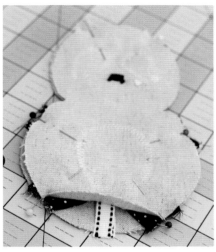

Figure A

6. Starting at the tail of the panda, lift the top front body piece so it is out of the way and stitch to attach the tail onto the back body. This section will be left open for turning and stuffing.

7. Stitch around the body, attaching the front and back bodies, leaving a 2″–3″ opening just at the tail. Turn the panda right side out.

8. Pull the tail out, stuff the body, and insert a small rattle in the center of the belly. Whipstitch the opening closed.

bunny

All seams are ¼˝ unless otherwise noted. Trace and cut out the bunny templates. Refer to Body Templates and Appliqué (page 30) and the bunny diagram (page 31) for making the body parts.

1. Place the ear fabrics right sides together in sets of 2. Place a piece of crinkle material on top of each set of ears.

2. Stitch around the curved edge of each set, leaving the straight side open for turning. Turn right side out.

3. Using a hand embroidery satin stitch, stitch the eyes on the bunny face.

4. Pin the ears and ribbon tail in place, with raw edges together, on the right side of the bunny back.

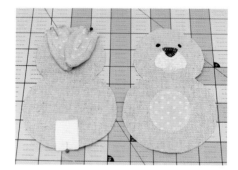

5. Place the bunny front piece right side together with the bunny back piece, covering all the little pieces tucked inside. Pin in place.

6. Starting at the tail of the bunny, lift the top front body piece so it is out of the way and stitch to attach the tail onto the back body. This section will be left open for turning and stuffing.

7. Stitch around the body to join the front and back body pieces, leaving a 2˝–3˝ opening just at the tail. Turn the bunny right side out.

8. Pull the tail out, stuff the body, and insert a small squeaker in the center of the belly. Whipstitch the opening closed.

owl

All seams are ¼˝ unless otherwise noted. Trace and cut out the owl templates. Refer to Body Templates and Appliqué (page 30) and the owl diagram (page 31) for making the body parts.

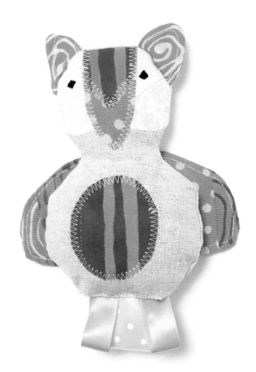

1. Place the ear fabrics right sides together in sets of 2. Place a piece of crinkle material on top of each set of ears.

2. Stitch around the curved edge of each set, leaving the straight side open for turning. Turn right side out.

3. Place the wing fabrics right sides together. Place a piece of crinkle material on top of one side.

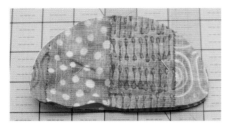

4. Stitch around all sides, leaving an approximately 3″ opening for turning. Turn right side out. Topstitch ⅛″ from the edge all around, closing the opening.

5. Center the wings on the back side of the owl body. Stitch a single line down the middle of the wings to attach them to the body back.

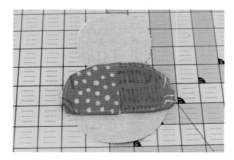

6. Fold and pin the wings toward the body's center so they do not get stitched into the outer seam. Pin the ears and ribbon tail in place, with raw edges together, on the right side of the owl back.

7. Using a hand embroidery satin stitch, stitch the eyes on the owl face.

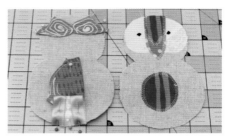

8. Place the owl front piece right side down on the owl back, covering all the little pieces tucked inside. Pin in place.

9. Starting at the tail of the owl, lift the top body piece so it is out of the way and stitch to attach the tail onto the body. This section will be left open for turning and stuffing.

10. Stitch around the body, leaving a 2″–3″ opening just at the tail. Turn the owl right side out.

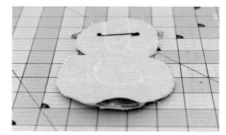

11. Pull the tail out, stuff the body, and insert a small rattle in the center of the belly. Whipstitch the opening closed.

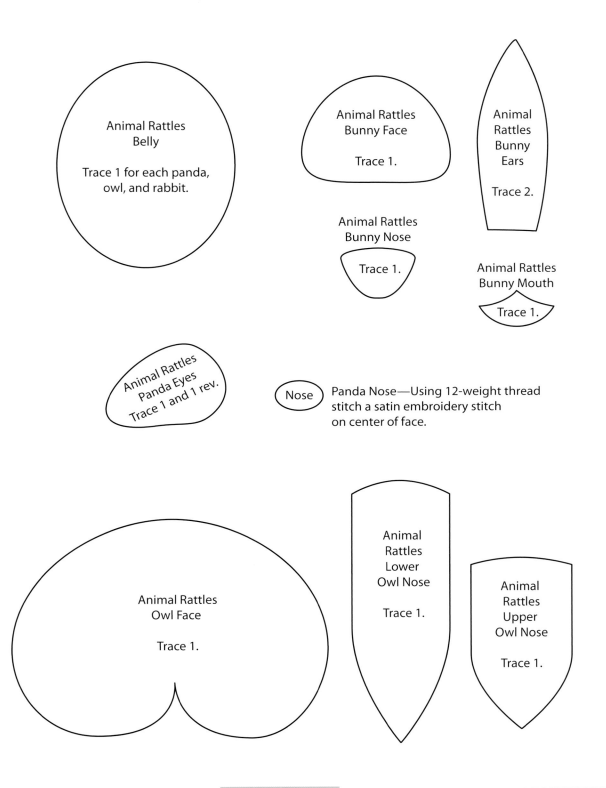

Animal Rattles
Belly

Trace 1 for each panda,
owl, and rabbit.

Animal Rattles
Bunny Face

Trace 1.

Animal
Rattles
Bunny
Ears

Trace 2.

Animal Rattles
Bunny Nose

Trace 1.

Animal Rattles
Bunny Mouth

Trace 1.

Animal Rattles
Panda Eyes
Trace 1 and 1 rev.

Nose

Panda Nose—Using 12-weight thread
stitch a satin embroidery stitch
on center of face.

Animal Rattles
Owl Face

Trace 1.

Animal
Rattles
Lower
Owl Nose

Trace 1.

Animal
Rattles
Upper
Owl Nose

Trace 1.

animal rattles

With Ollie's bright and spunky attitude, every child will want an Ollie of his or her own to hug and squeeze. Patchwork feathers and appliqués are stitched on and secure, so no worries of pieces falling off.

3 ollie the owl

Finished owl: *approximately 16″ tall*

- ½ yard of linen fabric

- 4 fabric scraps measuring no smaller than 3″ × 4″ each for the appliqués

- 236 fabric scraps measuring no smaller than 2½″ × 4″ each for the feathers

- ½ yard of fusible web

- 1 bag of polyester fiberfill

body templates and appliqués

Appliqué template patterns are on page 47 and main body part template patterns are on pullout page P1. Make and attach the appliqué pieces to the corresponding body parts before joining the body parts together.

1. Follow the cutting and tracing instructions on each pattern.

2. Cut the body and feet pieces from linen and the feather pieces from scrap fabrics.

3. Trace the appliqué templates on the paper side of the fusible web. Loosely cut around each of the traced shapes.

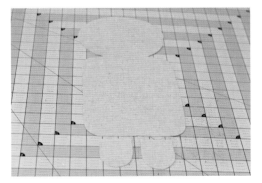

4. Position and press the adhesive side of the fusible web to the wrong side of your chosen fabric for the owl face. Cut along the traced lines.

5. Remove the paper backing and position the pieces on Ollie the Owl. Press in place.

6. Machine appliqué around each piece using your favorite stitch type. I chose a zigzag stitch.

instructions

All seams are ¼″ unless otherwise noted.

1. Place 2 feet pieces right sides together and stitch around the curved part of the foot, leaving the straight end open for turning and stuffing. Snip around the curve and turn right side out.

tip

Snipping or clipping the seam allowances around a curve, just up to the seam, will allow the seam to lie smooth rather than bunching up once the body is turned right side out.

2. Lightly stuff the feet and stitch a ⅛″ seam along the raw edge to close. Set aside.

3. Place 2 feather pieces right sides together and stitch around the curved part of the feather, leaving the straight end open for turning. Turn right side out. Press. Repeat this step to make 118 feathers.

4. Following the diagram, draw lines up the owl body front and back.

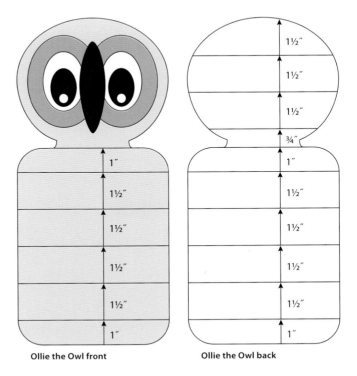

Ollie the Owl front · Ollie the Owl back

Measurements (front): 1″, 1½″, 1½″, 1½″, 1½″, 1″

Measurements (back): 1½″, 1½″, 1½″, ¾″, 1″, 1½″, 1½″, 1½″, 1″

5. On both the owl front and back, work from the bottom up to position 5 feathers, within a ¼″ seam allowance, facing upward along the first line. Stitch a horizontal seam along the raw edge and across the body piece, catching the feathers by ⅛″.

6. Fold the feathers down toward the bottom of the owl and topstitch ⅛″ from the edge to secure the feathers and hide the raw edges.

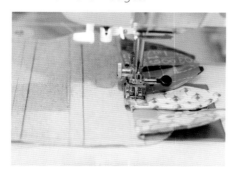

7. Repeat Steps 5 and 6 until all the lines on the owl front and back bodies (from the neck down) are covered in feathers. Overlap the feathers as you like, and use about 70–80 on the body.

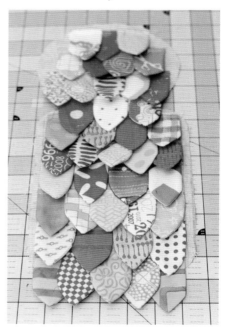

8. Add approximately 28–38 feathers to the back of the head in the same fashion as you attached them to the body. Add a few feathers to the face (about 4–6), lining up the raw edges with the head top, and pin in place. Leave a few feathers for covering the side seams (Step 14).

9. Fold in any layers of feathers that might get caught in the outside seam and pin.

10. Position the feet on the front bottom raw edge and pin inward toward the body of the owl.

11. Place the back and front body pieces right sides together. Keep all the feathers contained within the 2 pieces so they do not get caught in a seam. Use a few pins if needed, but be careful when turning the body right side out (Step 13).

12. Stitch along all the raw edges of the body to join the front to the back, leaving a 3″–4″ opening on one side.

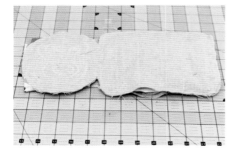

13. Turn the owl right side out and remove all the pins that held the feathers in place. Stuff the owl with fiberfill and whipstitch the opening closed.

14. Hand stitch the leftover feathers in place along the side seams of the body and face and anywhere else that needs filling in to give your Ollie an extra bit of spunk.

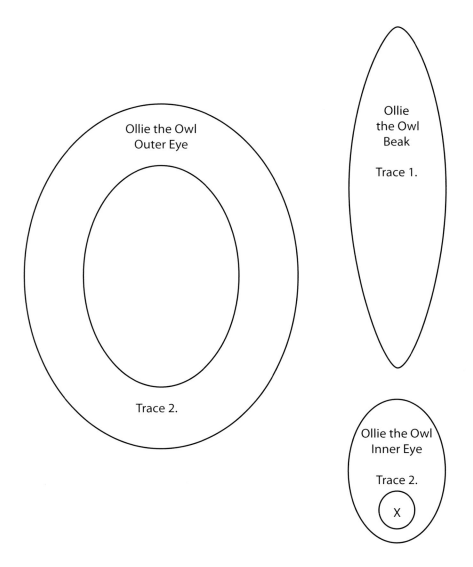

Ollie the Owl
Outer Eye

Trace 2.

Ollie
the Owl
Beak

Trace 1.

Ollie the Owl
Inner Eye

Trace 2.

X

Babies will love these soft oversized blocks as they shake, rattle, and roll them around the floor. High-contrast colors and numbers make these blocks a great learning toy that can be used throughout the toddler years.

4 shake, rattle, and roll jumbo blocks

Finished blocks: *approximately 10″, 7½″, and 5″*

MATERIALS

(For 1 block of each size; 3 total)

- ¾ yard of linen
- 2 squares 5″ × 5″ of fabric
- 2 squares 7½″ × 7½″ of fabric
- 2 squares 10″ × 10″ of fabric
- Various fabric scraps no larger than 10″ × 10″
- ¾ yard of fusible web
- 1⅛ yards of fusible fleece

- 2 bags of polyester fiberfill
- 1 large rattle insert for 10″ block
- 1 medium rattle insert for 7″ block
- 1 jingle bell insert for 5″ block
- 1⅝ yards each of ⅞″-wide and 1½″-wide ribbon
- Coordinating thread, 30-weight for embroidery and 50-weight for project construction

CUTTING

10″ block
- 4 squares 10″ × 10″ of linen
- 2 squares 10″ × 10″ of coordinating prints
- 6 squares 10″ × 10″ of fusible fleece

7½″ block
- 4 squares 7½″ × 7½″ of linen
- 2 squares 7½″ × 7½″ of coordinating prints
- 6 squares 7½″ × 7½″ of fusible fleece

5″ block
- 4 squares 5″ × 5″ of linen
- 2 squares 5″ × 5″ of coordinating prints
- 6 squares 5″ × 5″ of fusible fleece

instructions

Template patterns are on pages 53–57.

APPLIQUÉ TEMPLATES

1. Press the fusible fleece squares to the wrong sides of the print squares of the same size to make the appliqué backgrounds.

2. Follow the tracing instructions on each appliqué pattern.

3. Trace the appliqué templates on the paper side of the fusible web. Loosely cut around each of the traced shapes.

4. Position and press the adhesive side of the fusible web to the wrong side of the fabric scraps for the corresponding block templates. Cut along the traced lines.

5. Remove the paper backing and, referring to the diagrams below, center the pieces on each linen square for each block as instructed. Press in place. On the large block squares, place the letter a, number 1, 1 domino circle, and the apple. On the medium block squares, place the letter b, number 2, 2 domino circles, and the butterfly. On the small block squares, place the letter c, number 3, 3 domino circles, and the caterpillar.

Large block apple

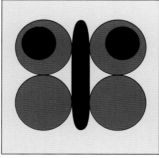

Medium block butterfly

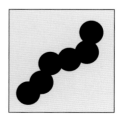

Small block caterpillar

6. Layer the individual appliqué pieces as needed and machine appliqué around each piece using your favorite stitch type. I chose a zigzag stitch.

7. Add any hand stitching details you would like to make the block unique.

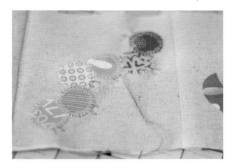

ASSEMBLING THE BLOCKS

All seams are ¼˝ unless otherwise noted.

1. From the ribbon, cut 6 pieces 3˝ long for each block (18 total if you are making all 3 blocks). Fold each piece of ribbon in half crosswise, matching the raw edges. Stitch with a ⅛˝ seam to hold the raw edges in place.

2. Make sure all the appliqué designs are facing the same direction. Pin 2 linen squares of the same size right sides together, sandwiching a piece of ribbon, and stitch along one side. Start and stop stitching ¼˝ from each end and back-stitch. Continue to add ribbons in the seams and stitch the linen squares until all 4 squares are stitched together in a single "flat" row.

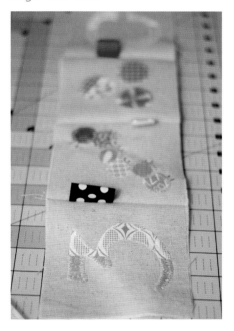

 note

The ribbon placement in each seam is random and is left to your discretion.

3. Take a row of 4 linen squares and place the 2 end squares right sides together. Sandwich a piece of ribbon in the seam and stitch to create the outside walls of the block. Start and stop stitching ¼˝ from each end and backstitch.

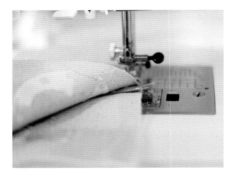

4. Pin the top square right sides together along the top side of the block and stitch in place along all 4 edges. Start and stop stitching with a backstitch ¼˝ from the ends of each seam. If you wish to add additional ribbon tags to the top, sandwich them into the seams where desired before stitching the top on.

5. Turn the block over and pin the bottom square right sides together along the bottom side of the block. Stitch into place as in Step 4. Leave a 3˝ opening along one side for turning and stuffing.

6. Turn the block right side out and stuff with fiberfill through the opening. Add a rattle or bell insert to the center of the block, surrounded by the stuffing. Whipstitch the opening closed.

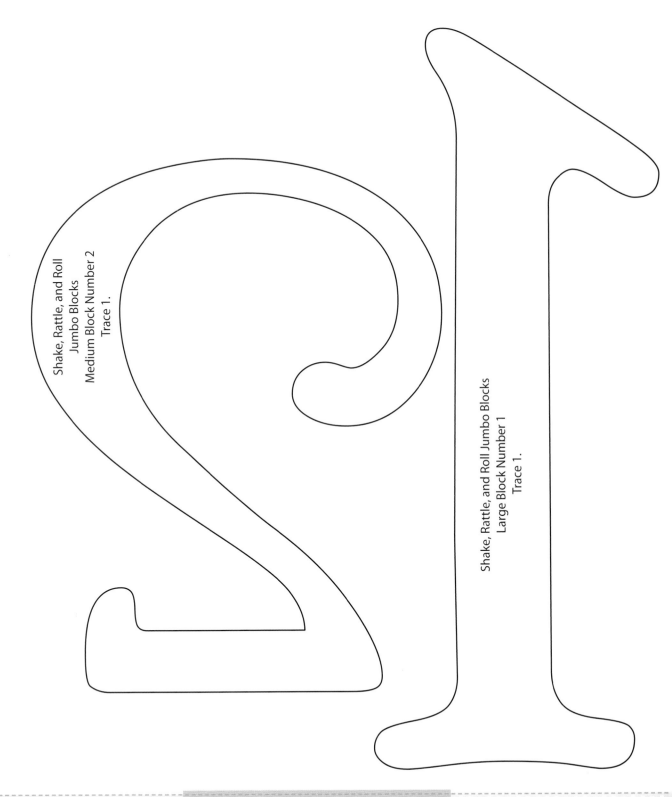

Shake, Rattle, and Roll
Jumbo Blocks
Medium Block Number 2
Trace 1.

Shake, Rattle, and Roll Jumbo Blocks
Large Block Number 1
Trace 1.

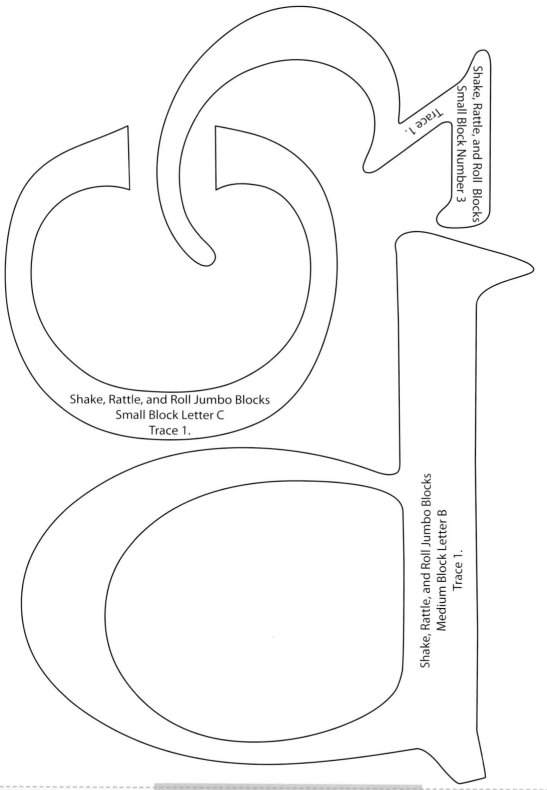

Shake, Rattle, and Roll Blocks
Small Block Number 3
Trace 1.

Shake, Rattle, and Roll Jumbo Blocks
Small Block Letter C
Trace 1.

Shake, Rattle, and Roll Jumbo Blocks
Medium Block Letter B
Trace 1.

shake, rattle, and roll jumbo blocks

Shake, Rattle, and Roll Jumbo Blocks
Large Block Letter A
Trace 1.

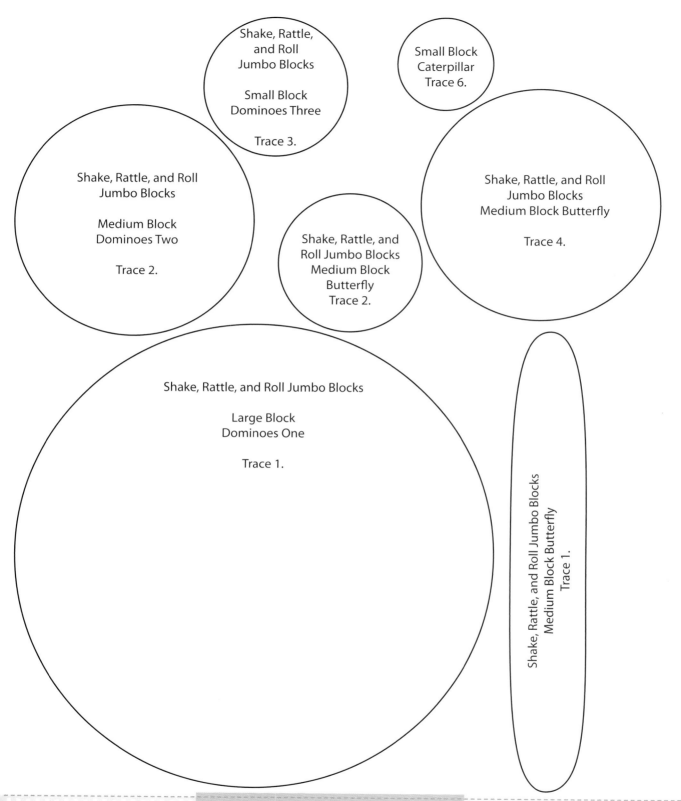

Shake, Rattle,
and Roll
Jumbo Blocks

Small Block
Dominoes Three

Trace 3.

Small Block
Caterpillar
Trace 6.

Shake, Rattle, and Roll
Jumbo Blocks

Medium Block
Dominoes Two

Trace 2.

Shake, Rattle, and
Roll Jumbo Blocks
Medium Block
Butterfly
Trace 2.

Shake, Rattle, and Roll
Jumbo Blocks
Medium Block Butterfly

Trace 4.

Shake, Rattle, and Roll Jumbo Blocks

Large Block
Dominoes One

Trace 1.

Shake, Rattle, and Roll Jumbo Blocks
Medium Block Butterfly
Trace 1.

shake, rattle, and roll jumbo blocks

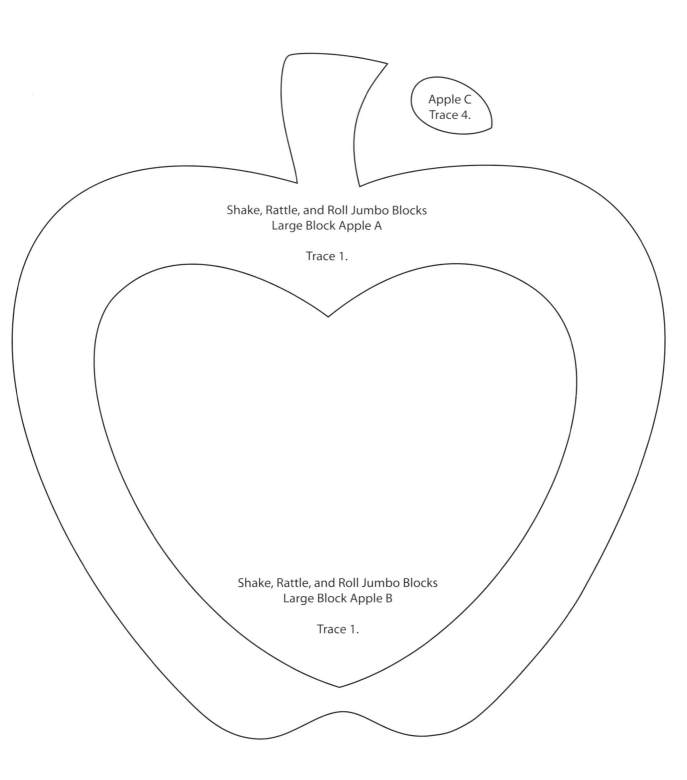

Apple C
Trace 4.

Shake, Rattle, and Roll Jumbo Blocks
Large Block Apple A

Trace 1.

Shake, Rattle, and Roll Jumbo Blocks
Large Block Apple B

Trace 1.

A fun and colorful design inspired by the traditional game of jacks. Bold colors offset by neutral linen and hand-stitched details make this quilt playful and energetic.

5 playing jacks quilt

Quilted by Natalia Bonner   **Finished quilt:** *47½″ × 66½″*

WOF = width of fabric

- 2⅛ yards of linen fabric

- 17 squares 10″ × 10″ of colored prints in reds, yellows, greens, teals, and oranges

- 32 strips 2½″ × WOF:

    4 strips each of reds, yellows, greens, teals, and oranges

    12 strips of grays

- 6 yards of fusible web

- 3¼ yards of coordinating fabric for the backing

- ⅝ yard of coordinating fabric for the binding

- 56″ × 75″ quilt batting

- Coordinating thread, 12-weight for embroidery and 50-weight for project construction

quilt top

All seams are ¼″ unless otherwise noted.
Template patterns are on pages 62 and 63.

1. Cut 18 squares 10″ × 10″ from linen.

2. Stitch the 2½″ × WOF strips side by side, grouped by color. For example, stitch all the red strips together, all the yellows together, all the grays together, and so on. Press all the seams in the same direction.

3. Trace the 35 circle and 24 jack templates onto the paper side of the fusible web. Loosely cut out.

4. Fuse 18 circle templates onto the wrong side of the colored strip-pieced fabrics as follows: 4 red, 4 yellow, 3 green, 4 teal, 3 orange.

5. Fuse the remaining 17 circle templates onto the wrong side of the linen fabric that has not been cut yet.

6. Cut out all the circles from the colored and linen fabrics, along the lines of the templates.

7. Fuse all 24 jack templates onto the wrong side of the gray strip-pieced fabric. Cut out all the jacks. Set aside.

8. Remove the paper backing from all the linen and colored circles. Fuse the 18 colored circles onto the centers of the 10″ × 10″ square linen blocks. Fuse the 17 linen circles onto the centers of the 10″ × 10″ square colored blocks.

tip

Fold the squares and circles in half both ways to easily locate the centers of both pieces. Line up the creased lines on the circles and squares and press into place.

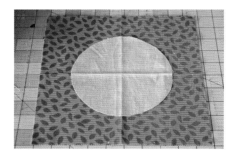

9. Machine appliqué the circles onto the squares using your favorite stitch type. I chose a small buttonhole stitch.

10. Using a 12-weight coordinating thread, hand stitch a decorative stitch around the insides of the linen circles.

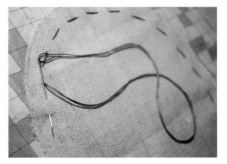

11. Stitch all the blocks together in rows, working from left to right. Press the seams in alternating directions from row to row. Continue until all the blocks are sewn together in rows.

12. Stitch all the rows together and press the seams in one direction to complete the quilt top.

13. Position and press the jack appliqués to the center of each cross section of blocks, as shown in the diagram.

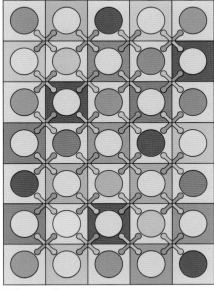

Quilt assembly

14. Machine appliqué around each jack using your favorite type of stitch. I chose a small buttonhole stitch.

FINISHING

1. The backing fabric should be approximately 4˝ larger than the quilt top on all 4 sides. Sandwich the quilt top, batting, and backing. Quilt as desired. I have my quilt tops quilted by a professional longarm quilter.

2. Use a rotary cutter, mat, and ruler to trim off any excess fabric from all sides of the quilt and square up the corners.

3. Cut 7 strips 2½˝ × width of fabric from the binding fabric. Trim all the selvages.

4. Finish your quilt by joining the binding strips together and adding the binding to the quilt. Refer to Binding (page 12) for step-by-step instructions.

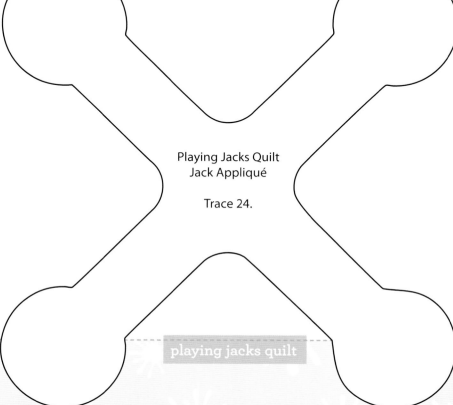

Playing Jacks Quilt
Jack Appliqué

Trace 24.

playing jacks quilt

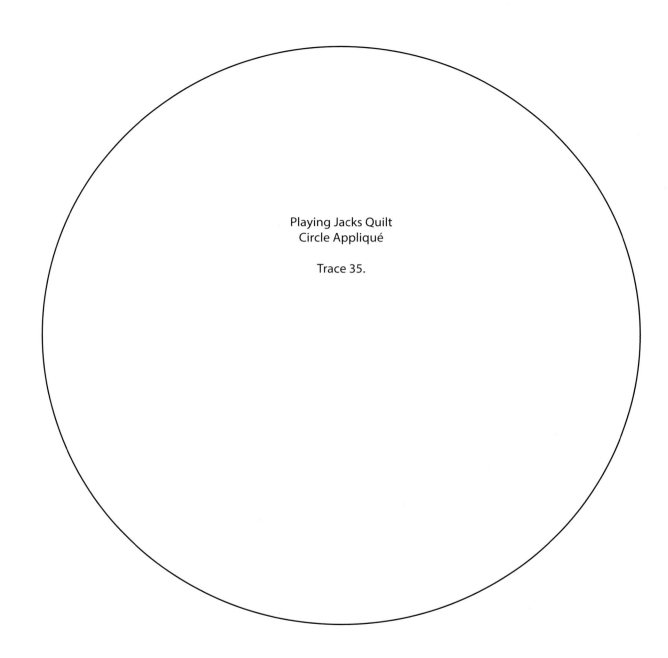

Playing Jacks Quilt
Circle Appliqué

Trace 35.

This carryall diaper bag has room for everything and is not just for the baby. It's great to use as an overnight bag, laptop bag, and more!

6 carryall bag

Finished bag: *approximately 23˝ wide × 18˝ high × 5½˝ deep*

MATERIALS

- 1⅜ yards of linen fabric for the exterior

- 2½ yards of print fabric for the interior

- 24 scraps 3½˝ × 3½˝ of print fabrics

- 1 yard of stabilizer

- 1⅞ yards of Shape-Flex interfacing (C&T Publishing)

- ¾ yard of Timtex interfacing (C&T Publishing)

- 1 magnetic snap ¾˝ in diameter

- 4 rectangle rings 1˝ wide

- 1½ yards of ½˝-wide elastic

- Coordinating thread, 12-weight for embroidery and 50-weight for project construction

- Safety pin or bodkin

CUTTING

From the exterior fabric:

- 18 rectangles 2½˝ × 3½˝

- 4 strips 2½˝ × 18½˝

- 8 strips 3˝ × 18½˝

- 2 rectangles 6½˝ × 18½˝ for the side panels

- 1 rectangle 6½˝ × 23½˝ for the bottom panel

- 4 rectangles 2˝ × 4˝ for the strap holders

- 2 strips 4˝ × 24˝ for the straps

From the interior fabric:

- 2 rectangles 18¼˝ × 23¼˝ for the front and back panels

- 2 rectangles 6¼˝ × 18¼˝ for the side panels

- 1 rectangle 6¼˝ × 23¼˝ for the bottom panel

- 2 rectangles 24˝ × 26¼˝ for the interior pockets

From the Shape-Flex:

- 2 rectangles 18½˝ × 23½˝ for the front and back panels

- 2 rectangles 6½˝ × 18½˝ for the side panels

- 2 rectangles 6½˝ × 23½˝ for the bottom panel

From the Timtex:

- 1 rectangle 5½˝ × 22½˝

From the stabilizer:

- 2 rectangles 18¼˝ × 23¼˝ for the front and back panels

- 2 rectangles 6¼˝ × 18¼˝ for the side panels

- 1 rectangle 6¼˝ × 23¼˝ for the bottom panel

instructions

BAG PIECING

All seams are ¼˝ unless otherwise noted.

1. Arrange 12 of the 3½˝ × 3½˝ squares from the scraps and 9 of the 2½˝ × 3½˝ exterior fabric rectangles in 3 rows, each with 4 squares and 3 rectangles. With right sides together, stitch together the rows. Press the seams toward the rectangles.

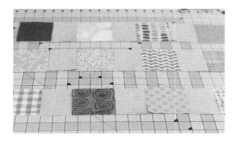

2. Stitch 2 exterior fabric strips 2½˝ × 18½˝ between the 3 rows, with right sides together. Press the seams toward the strips.

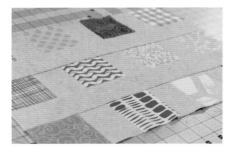

3. Stitch 1 exterior fabric strip 3˝ × 18½˝ to the top and 1 strip to the bottom of the pieced panel, with right sides together. Press the seams toward the strips.

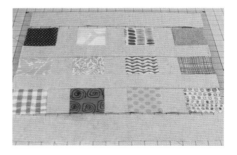

4. Stitch 1 exterior fabric strip 3˝ × 18½˝ to each side of the pieced panel, with right sides together. Press the seams toward the strips.

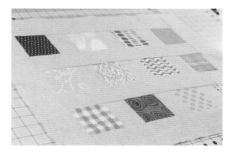

5. Using a 12-weight thread, hand stitch around each colored square with a corresponding thread color. I used a running stitch.

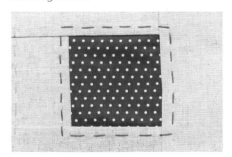

6. Repeat Steps 1–5 to create the other bag panel.

ATTACHING INTERFACINGS

1. Match the interior fabric cut pieces to the corresponding pieces of stabilizer. Stitch a ¼˝ seam around all the pieces to join and hold the stabilizer in place. Note that the lining pocket rectangles have no stabilizer rectangles.

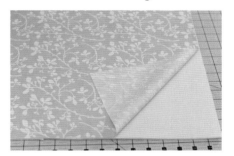

2. Following the manufacturer's instructions, fuse the Shape-Flex interfacing to the wrong side of the corresponding exterior pieces (including the pieced panels), matching up the sizes. You will have 1 piece of Shape-Flex interfacing left over.

3. Layer the heavyweight interfacing centered on the wrong side of the interfaced bottom exterior panel. Place the remaining piece of Shape-Flex interfacing fusible side down on top of the Timtex interfacing. Fuse all the pieces into place.

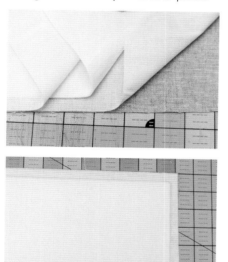

ASSEMBLY

Interior Pockets

1. Fold the large pocket panel in half, with wrong sides facing, to make a 12″ × 26¼″ rectangle. Press and top-stitch 1″ from the fold. Repeat for the second pocket panel.

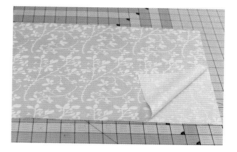

2. Fold the pocket panels in half (perpendicular to the first fold) to find the center of the pocket. Mark with a pin 1½″ on each side of the center fold.

3. Fold the pin marks in to the center fold and pin in place. Do this for both pocket panels.

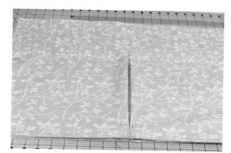

4. Align the raw edges of the pocket panel with the front or back interior panel, wrong side of pocket to right side of panel. Stitch ¼˝ in along the long bottom edge, securing the pleat in place. Repeat for the second panel.

5. Cut 2 pieces of elastic, each 23˝ long. Using a safety pin or bodkin, slip the elastic through the 1˝ casing on the pocket panels.

6. Align and pin the side raw edges and elastic ends in place on both interior panels. Stitch a ¼˝ seam along the side raw edges to secure the pocket and elastic.

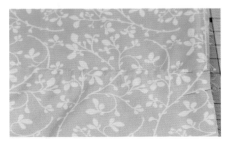

7. *Optional:* Stitch a straight seam down the center of each pocket to create 2 pockets on each panel.

Interior

All seams in this section are ½˝ unless otherwise noted.

1. Place the front or back interior panel and both interior side panels right sides together. Pin the side edges. Stitch all the side seams with a ½˝ seam, back-stitching and stopping ½˝ from the bottom edge.

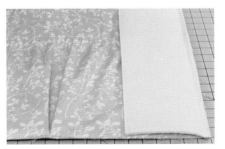

2. Repeat Step 1 to attach the remaining interior panel to the opposite side.

3. Place the bottom edge of the interior front and back panels and the long edge of the interior bottom panel right sides together. Pin along both long sides. Stitch a ½″ seam, starting and stopping ½″ from either end. (Backstitch at both ends.)

4. Match the short sides like you did with the long sides in Step 3 and pin. Stitch a ½″ seam along each side, starting and stopping ½″ from each end and backstitching.

5. Carefully trim the seam allowances to ¼″ on all interior edges of the bag, to reduce bulk.

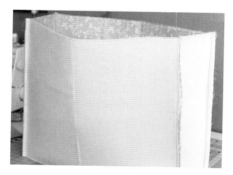

6. Following the manufacturer's instructions, attach the snaps at the center and 1½″ from the top on both the front and back interior panels. Set aside.

Exterior

1. Place the first main exterior panel and both of the exterior side panels right sides facing. Pin the side edges. Stitch a ½″ seam, stopping and backstitching ½″ from the bottom edge.

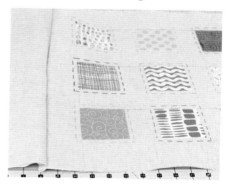

2. Repeat Step 1 to attach the second main exterior panel to the opposite side of the side panels.

3. Place the bottom edge of the exterior main panels and the long edge of the exterior bottom panel right sides facing. Pin along both sides. Stitch a ½″ seam, starting and stopping ½″ from either end. Backstitch at each end.

4. Match the short sides like you did with the long sides in Step 3 and pin. Stitch a ½″ seam along each side, stopping ½″ from each end and backstitching.

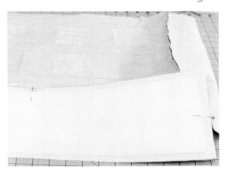

5. Carefully trim the seam allowances to ¼″ on all sides of the bag to reduce bulk. Turn the exterior bag right side out.

finishing

1. Fold an exterior fabric rectangle 2″ × 4″ in half crosswise to make a crease. Unfold. Fold the 2 short ends toward the center crease and fold again along the first crease. Topstitch along both new long edges to secure in place. Repeat to make 4.

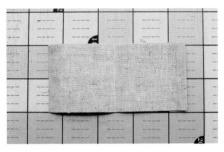

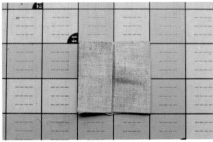

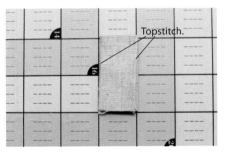

Topstitch.

2. Fold an exterior fabric strip 4″ × 24″ in half lengthwise, crease, and unfold. Fold the long edges to the center and crease. Fold in half again on the first crease. Topstitch along both long edges to make a 24″-long strap. Zigzag stitch the raw ends to finish. Repeat to make 2.

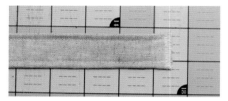

3. Slip a 2″ strap piece from Step 1 through the rectangle rings, matching the raw edges together. Stitch a ⅛″ seam to hold in place. Repeat for all 4 rings.

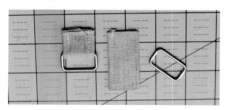

4. Place the exterior bag in the interior bag, with right sides facing. Pin the top raw edges together.

5. Position the 4 strap rings (from Step 3) 4″ from each of the 4 bag side seams along the top of the 2 main panels. Match the strap ring raw edges with the top of the main panel and then point the rings down so they are sandwiched between the exterior and interior panels.

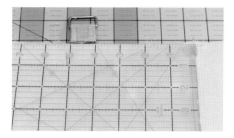

6. Stitch a ½″ seam allowance along the top of the bag, leaving a 4″–6″ opening on the front side of the bag. Turn the bag right side out through the opening.

7. Push the bag interior down into the bag exterior. Press the top seam and pin the opening closed.

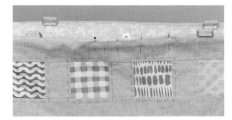

8. Topstitch the top of the bag to close the opening.

9. Making sure the strap is not twisted, slip the long strap ends through the rings and stitch the raw edges into place. Be sure to backstitch a couple of times to strengthen the seam.

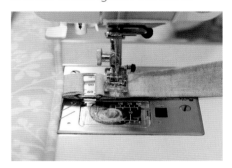

No more digging all through your purse or diaper bag trying to find the reward card or membership card for purchases. Keep all your important or regularly used cards, whether they are reward cards, credit cards, or membership cards, tucked securely away in this compact card holder.

7 card holder

Finished holder: *3½″ wide × 4″ high × ¾″ deep*

MATERIALS

- ¼ yard of linen fabric
- 2½″ × 4½″ rectangle of scrap fabric
- 4½″ × 7½″ rectangle of fast2fuse medium interfacing
- Coordinating thread, 12-weight for embroidery and 50-weight for project construction
- 2 large eyelets
- ¾″ aluminum threaded post with screw
- 12 name badge, ID, or picture/card holders, 2¼″ × 3½″
- Single-hole punch

CUTTING

- 2 rectangles 3″ × 4½″ of linen fabric
- 1 rectangle 4½″ × 7½″ of linen fabric

instructions

All seams are ¼″ unless otherwise noted.

1. Stitch a 3″ × 4½″ linen rectangle on each side of the 2½″ × 4½″ rectangle of scrap fabric. Press.

2. Use a contrasting 12-weight thread and hand stitch on either side of the scrap fabric.

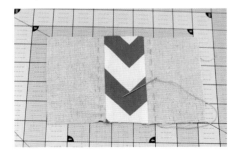

3. Fuse the fast2fuse interfacing to the wrong side of the 4½″ × 7½″ rectangle of linen.

4. Arrange the pieced exterior and interior pieces of fabric with right sides facing.

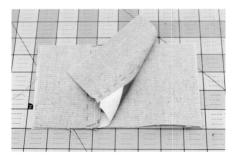

5. Stitch around all 4 sides, leaving a 3″ opening for turning. Clip the corners.

6. Turn right side out and topstitch ⅛″ from the edge on all 4 sides, closing up the opening.

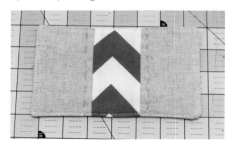

7. Following the manufacturer's instructions, attach eyelets at the top corners of both sides, centered about ½″ from the corners.

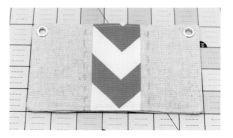

8. Place a plastic badge sleeve with the opening at the center of the fabric, aligning the outside edges. Use a pen to mark the center of the eyelet hole on the plastic sleeve. Punch the hole through the plastic sleeve with a single-hole punch and use this badge sleeve as a template to punch out the remaining 11 sleeves.

9. Push the threaded post through the front of the card holder and continue through the holes of the 12 sleeves and finally through the back of the card holder eyelet. Twist in the screw to complete the holder.

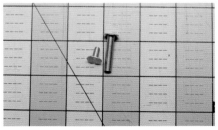

This woven-inspired pattern made in high-contrast black and white solid fabrics creates a fun yet sophisticated look that every mom will love to tote around.

8 opposites attract quilt

Quilted by Natalia Bonner   **Finished quilt:** *58″ × 70″*

MATERIALS

- 1 white solid 2½″-strip bundle *or* 2 yards of white fabric

- 1 black solid 2½″-strip bundle *or* 2¾ yards of black fabric

- 8 panels of 2½″-grid interfacing (Quiltsmart Watercolor 2½″ Grid Interfacing)

- 3⅞ yards of coordinating fabric for the backing

- ⅝ yard of coordinating fabric for the binding

- 66″ × 78″ quilt batting

CUTTING

Cut 1,015 squares 2½″ × 2½″ from strip bundles or yardage:

- Black: 595 squares

- White: 420 squares

> ✳ **note**
>
> *You can get 16 squares 2½″ × 2½″ from each strip-bundle strip (2½″ × width of fabric).*

quilt top

All seams are ¼″ unless otherwise noted.

1. Separate the interfacing panels into individual pieces. You should have 8 panels total. Trim the instruction border from each interfacing panel. Don't remove the partial squares on the perimeter and leave a slight border all around.

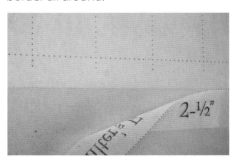

2. Arrange the widest part of the interfacing panels across the width of the quilt. Use the diagram as a guide to place and fuse the squares to the 8 panels. Three of the panels are 14 squares wide × 9 squares high, and 3 are 15 squares wide × 9 squares high, while 1 bottom panel is 14 × 8 squares high and the other is 15 × 8 squares high.

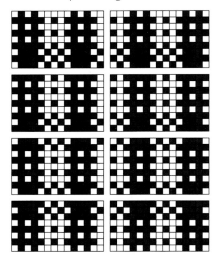

3. Working from left to right and top to bottom of the first upper left panel, fuse the squares in place on the grid, following the manufacturer's instructions.

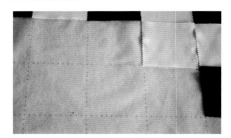

4. After you have the first panel filled, attach the next panel to the bottom by aligning the squares and fusing them into place.

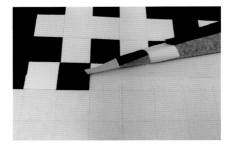

5. When you are finished fusing all the squares and adjoining each panel as you go, you should have a large panel of squares that looks like this diagram.

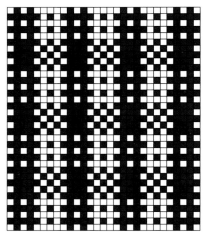

Quilt diagram

6. Working a row at a time, carefully fold and stitch the rows right sides together at the crease. Continue until all the rows are sewn together. Then turn and sew all the columns together just like you did the rows.

7. When you are finished stitching all the rows and columns together, press the seams in one direction to complete the quilt top.

 tip

■ Fusing squares to a grid interfacing will help make your design come together quickly and easily. Several grid sizes are available to fit to any application you wish to use. This also helps keep all the seams lined up nicely when you are sewing them together.

■ Optionally, to reduce bulk at the seams after stitching the rows, trim the grid interfacing on the fold lines of the rows and open up the seams and press them flat. Repeat after the columns are sewn.

finishing

1. The backing fabric should be about 4˝ larger than the quilt top on all 4 sides. Sandwich the quilt top, batting, and backing. Quilt as desired. I have my quilt tops quilted by a professional longarm quilter.

2. Use a rotary cutter, mat, and ruler to trim any excess fabric from all 4 sides of the quilt and square up the corners.

3. From the binding fabric, cut 8 strips 2½˝ × width of fabric. Trim all the selvages.

4. Finish your quilt by joining the binding strips together and adding the binding to the quilt. Refer to Binding (page 12) for step-by-step instructions.

Look fabulous while nursing your child with this cute cover-up. Features include a hidden pocket to store your phone or pacifier while feeding baby and a moldable curved neck to allow you to keep an eye on your little one. You also can keep track of which side you fed from previously by attaching a clippie (page 88) to the right or left side of the neck strap.

9 nursing cover-up

Finished cover-up: *34″ × 24″*

MATERIALS

- 1 yard of linen
- 1 yard of fabric for the backing
- 12 rectangles 2½″ × 6½″ of scrap fabric
- ¼″ Featherlite boning, 16″ long
- Overall buckle with no-sew button

CUTTING

From the linen:

- 1 rectangle 21½″ × 24½″ for the front left
- 1 rectangle 7½″ × 24½″ for the front right
- 2 rectangles 7½″ × 8½″ for the pocket

From the backing fabric:

- 1 rectangle 24½″ × 34½″ for the back
- 1 rectangle 6″ × 34½″ for the strap

instructions

All seams are ¼″ unless otherwise noted.

1. Stitch the 12 pieces of scrap fabric together along the 6½″ sides to make a scrap strip measuring 6½″ × 24½″. Press.

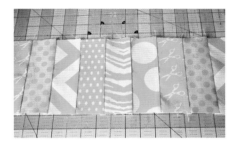

2. To make the front cover, with right sides facing, stitch the 21½″ × 24½″ linen rectangle to the left side of the 6½″ × 24½″ scrap strip. Next stitch the 7½″ × 24½″ linen rectangle to the right side of the scrap strip.

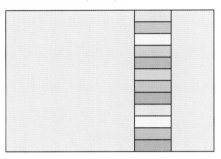

3. On the outside of the front cover, position and pin the 8½″ (wrong) side of a linen pocket piece 2″ from the bottom of the front cover, along the left edge of the front cover. Stitch in place. Clip the seam allowance of the front cover on each side of the pocket. Press the seams toward the cover and topstitch ⅛″ from the seam.

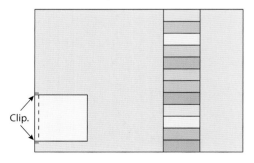

Clip.

4. Position and pin the 8½″ (wrong) side of the second linen pocket piece 2″ from the bottom, along the outside right edge of the backing piece. Stitch in place. Clip the backing seam allowance on each side of the pocket. Press the seams toward the backing and topstitch ⅛″ from the seam.

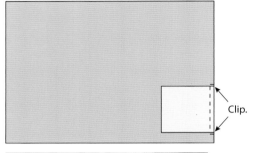

Clip.

5. Fold the 6″ × 34½″ strap piece of fabric in half lengthwise, wrong sides together, and crease. Open the piece back up and fold the raw edges toward the centerfold. Fold a short end in ½″; then fold the strap in half lengthwise along the first fold again and topstitch the 3 folded sides closed.

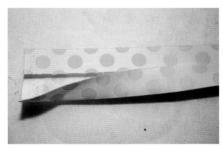

6. Place the front and back pieces of the cover right sides together. Pocket pieces should align and protrude. Pin in place. Aligning a raw edge of the strap with the top of the cover, sandwich the strap between the 2 pieces of the nursing cover, 9″ from the side edge of the front (so the strap is located near the middle of the pieced strip). Catching the raw end of the strap, stitch around all the raw edges of the nursing cover *except* for the bottom. When you reach the pocket, pivot and stitch along 3 pocket edges; then pivot and continue stitching the side seam of the nursing cover. Leave the bottom open for turning and inserting the boning at the neck.

7. Turn the nursing cover right side out and topstitch along the top. Push the pocket in between the front and back layers of the nursing cover.

8. On the cover front, measure in 9″ from both sides and down 1″ from the top. Mark both places with a pin. Starting at the top edge, stitch down 1″ from the top seam to each pin, resulting in 2 stitched marks. The stitching goes through both layers of the nursing cover.

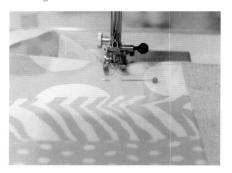

9. Entering from the bottom of the piece, insert the 16″ piece of boning in the top center of the cover, just between the 2 stitched marks made in Step 8. Pin in place.

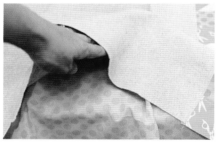

10. Stitch all the way across the cover, parallel to the top edge and 1˝ down from the top of the cover, to secure the boning.

11. Fold the bottom hem ¼˝ in toward the wrong side on both the front and back pieces. Pin together and topstitch ⅛˝ from the edge to close the bottom hem. Topstitch on the right side. On the left side, topstitch skipping over the pocket opening.

12. Follow the manufacturer's instructions to position and attach the strap to the buckle and the no-sew button to the left of the end of the boning.

13. Attach a clippie (page 88) for added flair and to mark which side to feed on.

Make this super-simple clippie that you can attach to clothing, the Nursing Cover-Up (page 82), hair ... just about anywhere.

10

clippie

MATERIALS

- ¼ yard of linen fabric
- Contrasting button ½˝ in diameter
- Alligator clip

instructions

Template pattern is on pullout page P1.

1. Use the flower template to cut 5 linen flowers.

2. Fold a flower in half twice. Repeat for 3 more flowers.

3. Place the 4 folded flowers on the remaining flower, matching up the points in the center.

4. Stitch an X in the center to tack the centers to the base flower. Each arm is about 1˝ long, centered.

5. Crinkle or squish the flower in your hand to ruffle up the layers.

6. Hand stitch a decorative button in the center.

7. Hand stitch an alligator clip to the back.

11 | BIB

This adorable terry cloth and knit fabric baby bib slips quickly and easily over baby's head without messing around with snaps or hook-and-loop tape. The soft fabrics are gentle on a baby's face when it's time to clean up.

11 bib

MATERIALS

- Terry cloth hand towel
- ½ yard of knit fabric
- 2 adult knitted cuffs (Dritz 55415-9)
- 4″ × 8″ piece of paper-backed fusible web

instructions

Templates are on page 95.

1. Cut both the terry cloth towel and knit fabric to 11″ × 14½″. Set aside.

2. Trace the *eat.* pattern template on the paper side of the fusible web. Loosely cut around the letters and fuse to the wrong side of the piece of knit fabric. Cut out the letters.

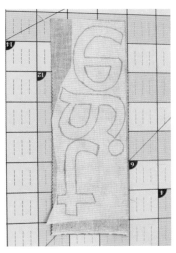

3. Remove the paper backing from the letters and press to the front side of the terry cloth, 2″ from the bottom and right side.

4. Stitch the appliqués on with your favorite stitch. I made random straight stitches following the shapes of the letters.

5. Match the terry cloth and knit fabric pieces right sides together and stitch a ¼˝ seam around all 4 sides. *Do not leave an opening.*

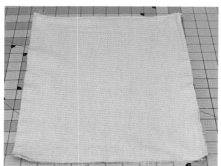

6. Trace the circle pattern and center the circle template 1½˝ down from the top of the fabric rectangle. Carefully cut out the circle from both layers.

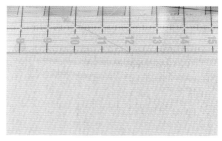

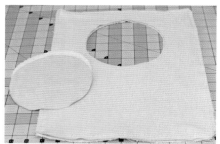

7. Turn the bib right side out. Press and topstitch ⅛″ from the edge around all 4 sides of the bib.

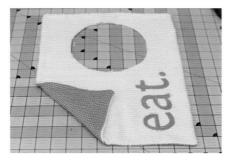

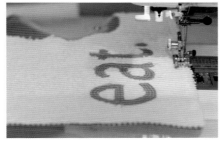

8. Cut each knitted cuff 1½″ from the top fold to remove excess.

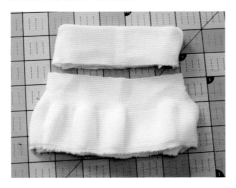

9. Open the fold and cut crosswise (perpendicular to the fold) to open the cuff. The piece measures about 3″ × 5″. Repeat this step for the second cuff. Place the 2 pieces right sides together and stitch or serge a ¼″ seam connecting both sets of short ends. This will become the knit collar.

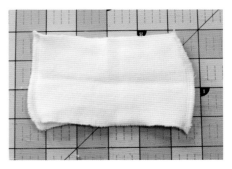

10. Fold and press the knit collar in half lengthwise, with wrong sides together.

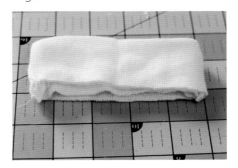

11. Fold the bib so the top and bottom circle edges are aligned and put a pin at the left and right circle edges. With right sides together, pin the side raw edges of the collar to the side left and right edges of the neck cutout.

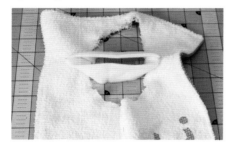

12. Repeat Step 11 for the top and bottom of the collar.

tip

Stretch the collar while serging or zigzag stitching it to the neck between each pinned location. This will ensure that the collar will be even all the way around the neck and will lie flat.

13. Serge or zigzag the collar to the bib.

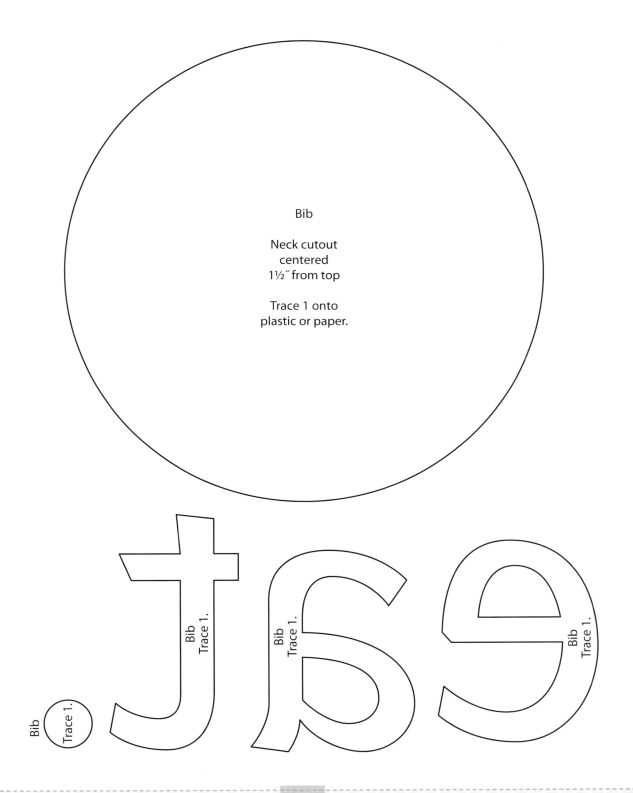

Bib

Neck cutout
centered
1½″ from top

Trace 1 onto
plastic or paper.

Bib
Trace 1.

Bib
Trace 1.

Bib
Trace 1.

Bib
Trace 1.

Embellish plain cloth diapers with fabric to create a simple, quick gift that any mom would love to receive.

12

burp cloth

MATERIALS

- 1 fat eighth of cotton fabric per burp cloth

- 1 cloth diaper per burp cloth, approximately 13½″ × 19″ with absorbent padding in the center

instructions

All seams are ¼″ unless otherwise noted.

1. Cut 6″ × 22″ from the fat eighth fabric.

2. Press the fabric and cloth diaper.

3. Fold and press ½″ toward the wrong side of the fabric along the longest edges.

4. Fold and press 1″ or more on the short ends toward the wrong side of the fabric to fit the cloth diaper.

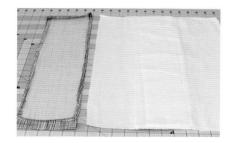

5. Center and pin the fabric to the middle of the burp cloth, over the absorbent padding, with right sides facing up. Wrap the ends around to the back of the cloth diaper about ½˝ and zigzag stitch in place.

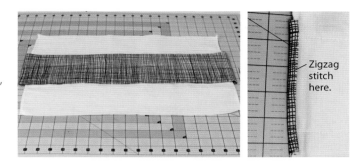

Zigzag stitch here.

6. Stitch ⅛˝ from all 4 edges of the fabric on the cloth diaper. Quilt the center as desired.

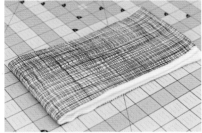

Be prepared to change your child no matter where you might be, and be stylish while doing it. This vinyl-coated changing pad easily wipes clean, has storage space for extra wipes and diapers, and sports a sophisticated look—all rolled up in one.

13 changing pad

Finished pad: *14″ × 38″*

MATERIALS

- ½ yard of exterior fabric
- ⅞ yard of interior fabric
- ½ yard of contrasting fabric for pocket
- 1 yard of clear vinyl (Quilter's Vinyl by C&T Publishing)
- 1 yard of fusible fleece
- 5″ × 5″ piece of fusible web
- 13″ piece of ⅜″-wide elastic
- 2 yards of ⅜″-wide grosgrain ribbon

CUTTING

From the exterior fabric:
- 1 piece 15″ × 31″

From the interior fabric:
- 1 piece 15″ × 31″
- 2 pieces 9″ × 13″

From the contrasting fabric:
- 1 piece 16″ × 16″

From the clear vinyl:
- 1 piece 15″ × 31″

From the fusible fleece:
- 1 piece 15″ × 31″
- 1 piece 9″ × 13″

instructions

All seams are ½″ unless otherwise noted.

1. Press the adhesive side of the 15″ × 31″ piece of fusible fleece to the wrong side of the exterior fabric.

2. Press the adhesive side of the 9″ × 13″ piece of fusible fleece to the wrong side of a 9″ × 13″ piece of interior fabric.

3. Fold the 16″ × 16″ piece of contrasting fabric in half, with wrong sides facing. Stitch ½″ from the folded edge. This will become the pocket.

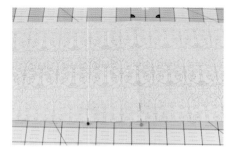

4. Fold the pocket in half crosswise, matching the 2 short raw edges, and crease the center. Open the pocket back up and place pins 1½″ on either side of the center fold.

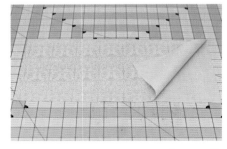

5. Fold the pocket at the pins and match the pleats to the center fold. Topstitch ⅛″ from the bottom raw edge to secure the pleats in place.

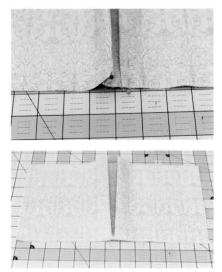

6. Using a bodkin or safety pin, slide the elastic through the casing on the pocket. Stitch the ends of the elastic in the casing.

7. Place the 9″ × 13″ piece of interior fabric with the fusible fleece on the back right side up. Next, place the pocket on the interior fabric, right side up, aligning the raw edges at the bottom and sides. Last, place the other 9″ × 13″ piece of interior fabric on top, with the right side down. Pin and stitch a ½″ seam around the bottom and sides. Clip the 2 bottom corners.

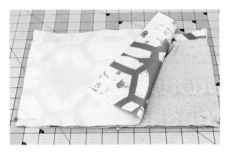

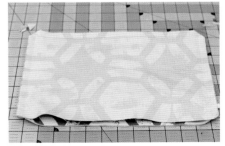

8. Turn the pocket right side out and topstitch ⅛″ from the edge along the sides and bottom.

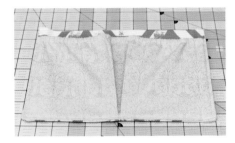

9. On a computer, create a letter using a font of your choice in a document or photo editor. The letter should measure about 4″–5″ high. Print the letter mirror imaged, and then trace it on the paper side of the fusible web. Loosely cut around the letter and fuse it to the wrong side of the contrasting fabric leftovers.

10. Cut out the letter and press it to the right-hand corner of the exterior fabric, 2″ from the bottom and side raw edges. Place the bottom of the letter parallel to the raw edge of the side measuring 15″. Machine appliqué with your favorite stitch.

11. Align the clear vinyl on top of the right side of the interior fabric piece 15″ × 31″. Carefully stitch ⅛″ from all the edges to prevent slipping when you are sewing the changing pad together.

12. Lay the exterior fabric right side up so that the fusible fleece is at the bottom. Next, center the pocket flap right side up on the opposite side of the letter appliqué, centering and matching the raw edges together. Last, align the vinyl-covered interior fabric right side down, sandwiching the pocket between the inside and outside layers. Pin in place.

13. Stitch a ½˝ seam around the 2 long sides and the side with the pocket flap. Do not stitch the short side with the letter appliqué. Clip the 2 corners on the stitched side.

14. Turn the changing pad right side out. *Do not* press the changing pad because the vinyl will melt. Topstitch ⅛˝ from the edge around the 3 stitched sides.

15. Straight stitch crosswise seams 10˝ and 20˝ from the side with the pocket.

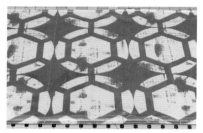

16. On the open end, fold the raw edges in toward the wrong sides of the fabrics and pin.

17. Cut the ribbon into 2 pieces, each 36˝ long. Place an end of one piece of ribbon on top of an end of the other, centered along the folded edges of the 2 pieces of fabric. Pin in place.

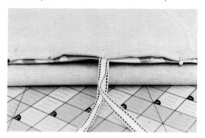

18. Topstitch ⅛˝ from the edge along the open end to close off the opening. Backstitch over the ribbon to secure in place.

19. Fill the pocket with wipes and diapers. Roll up the changing pad, wrap the ribbon around it, and tie off.

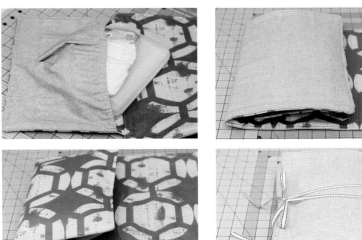

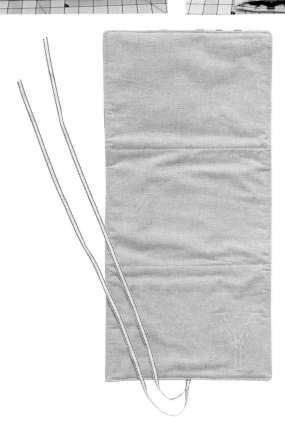

14 | BISCOTTI

What are biscotti? Well, we call the little pacifiers "biscuits," and when you add little blankets to them, they become biscotti. The permanently attached blanket and a pacifier can easily be thrown into the wash and hung up to dry.

14 biscotti

Finished biscotti: *10½″ × 13½″*

MATERIALS

- 11″ × 14″ piece of knit fabric
- 11″ × 14″ piece of contrasting knit fabric
- Shoelace
- Pacifier

instructions

All seams are ¼″ unless otherwise noted.

1. Place the 2 pieces of knit fabric right sides facing.

2. Serge or zigzag stitch to join the 2 pieces of knit fabrics together along 1 short and 2 long sides.

3. Turn the blanket right side out and fold the raw edges of both fabrics under ½″.

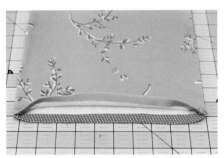

4. Topstitch the blanket on all 4 sides with ⅛″ and ¼″ seams. I used a cover-stitch machine to topstitch, but a straight stitch or other decorative stitch works fine.

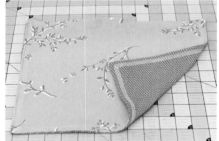

5. Weave the shoelace through the holes of the pacifier, starting on the side with the nipple.

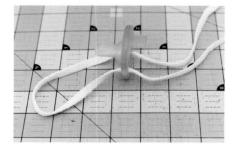

6. Pull the shoelace ends through the loop and pull until tight.

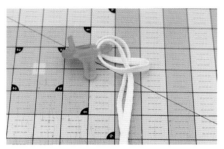

7. Trim the shoelace 1″ from the pacifier.

8. Find the center of the blanket and mark it.

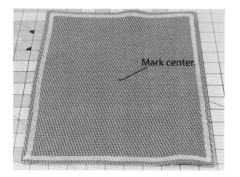

9. Make a small fold in the center of the blanket. Pin the ends of the shoelace in the fold at the center of the blanket.

10. Stitch and backstitch a short ¼" seam just to secure the ends of the shoelace in the blanket.

11. Turn the blanket to the opposite side and stitch short seams ⅛" and ⅜" away from the blanket fold.

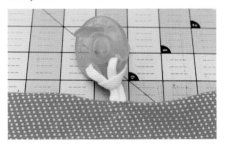

15 | TWEEDLE DEE QUILT

Inspired by the woven texture of tweed, this quilt features high-contrast red, white, and linen fabrics. The mixture of red half-square triangles with flat piping details and solid white squares makes this quilt a real eye-catcher.

15 tweedle dee quilt

Quilted by Natalia Bonner **Finished quilt:** *58½″ × 58½″*

MATERIALS

- 1½ yards of red dot fabric
- 1½ yards of red solid fabric
- 1¾ yards of white solid fabric
- ½ yard of linen
- 3⅞ yards of coordinating fabric for the backing
- ⅝ yard of coordinating fabric for the binding
- 67″ × 67″ quilt batting

CUTTING

From the red dot fabric:

- 16 squares 5″ × 5″
- 36 squares 5½″ × 5½″, subcut diagonally at a 45° angle

From the red solid fabric:

- 16 squares 5″ × 5″
- 40 squares 5½″ × 5½″, subcut diagonally at a 45° angle

From the white solid fabric:

- 49 squares 5″ × 5″
- 84 strips 1″ × 8½″

From the linen:

- 4 squares 5″ × 5″
- 8 squares 5½″ × 5½″, subcut diagonally at a 45° angle

quilt top

All seams are ¼″ unless otherwise noted.

1. Fold the 1″ × 8½″ strip in half lengthwise and press. Repeat this step for all 84 strips.

2. Matching raw edges, sandwich 1 white folded strip in between 2 red dot triangles, with right sides together. Stitch in place.

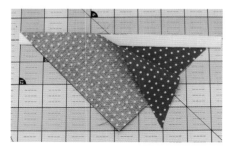

3. Open and press the seams in one direction. Square up the block to 5″ × 5″.

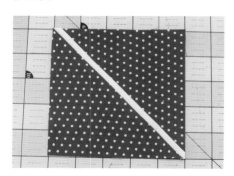

4. Repeat Steps 2 and 3 until you have the following blocks:

- 12 blocks with 2 red dot triangles

- 24 blocks with 2 red solid triangles

- 32 blocks with red dot and red solid triangles

- 16 blocks with red dot and linen triangles

5. Stitch together each row of blocks as shown in the diagram (page 111). Four different row combinations make up the design. Press the seams in alternate directions from row to row.

- 3 each of row 1

- 4 each of row 2

- 4 each of row 3 (2 rows have the half-square triangle units reversed)

- 2 each of row 4

6. Stitch all the rows together and press the seams in one direction to complete the quilt top.

Quilt assembly

finishing

1. The backing should be about 4˝ larger than the quilt top on all 4 sides. Sandwich the quilt top, batting, and backing. Quilt as desired. I have my quilt tops quilted by a professional longarm quilter.

2. Use a rotary cutter, mat, and ruler to trim excess fabric from all sides of the quilt and square up the corners.

3. Cut 7 strips 2½˝ × width of fabric from the binding fabric. Trim the selvages.

4. Finish your quilt by joining the binding strips together and adding the binding to the quilt. Refer to Binding (page 12) for step-by-step instructions.

Capture special moments such as an infant's monthly milestone or your child's birthday. Here are twelve adorable numbers that you can appliqué to any baby bodysuit or T-shirt.

16 1, 2 ... twelve— appliqué numbers

MATERIALS

- 1 bodysuit or T-shirt, any size

- Assorted fabric scraps to make an 8″ × 8″ fabric base square

- ¼ yard of fusible web

instructions

Please refer to page 11 for instructions for creating scrap appliqué.

Template patterns are on pages 114–120.

1. From colored scraps, sew strips together in groups, creating an 8″ × 8″ strip block.

2. Press the seams in the same direction. *Optional:* Topstitch the seams down.

3. For the selected number set, trace the template patterns on the paper side of the fusible web. Note that the letters come in 2 sizes, depending on the length of the word.

4. Loosely cut around each of the traced shapes. Position and press the traced shapes to the back of the colored 8″ × 8″ fabric. Cut out all the numbers and letters you selected.

5. Using the image as a guide for placement, fuse the appliqués in place to the front of the bodysuit or T-shirt.

6. Machine appliqué the pieces with your favorite stitch type. I used a small buttonhole stitch around all the pieces.

Trace the letters for the words *one, two, four, five, six,* and *ten.*

1, 2 … twelve—appliqué numbers

Trace the letters for the words *one, two, four, five, six,* **and** *ten.*

Trace the letters for the words *three*, *seven*, *eight*, *nine*, *eleven*, and *twelve*.

1, 2 … twelve—appliqué numbers

Number 2

Number 0

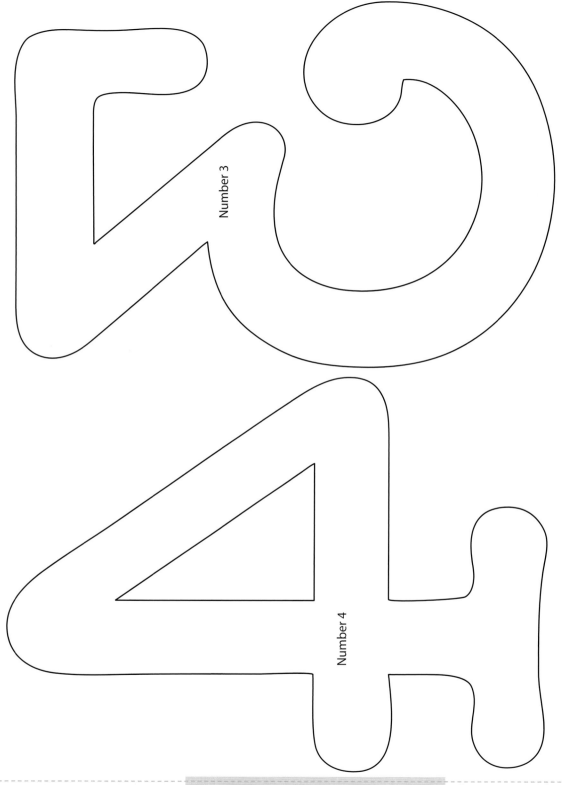

Number 3

Number 4

Number 5

Number 6
Number 9

Number 7

Number 8

Protect your baby from the sun, wind, rain, and more with this adorable carrier cover inspired by baby sprouts. Fun geometric shapes in fresh greens give this cover an organic feel.

17 baby sprouts carrier cover

Finished cover: *36˝ × 45˝*

MATERIALS

WOF = width of fabric

- 1½ yards of linen fabric
- 1½ yards of backing fabric
- 5˝ × WOF strips of 10 different green prints
- 1½ yards of fusible fleece
- 4⅝ yards of fusible web
- 1⅞ yards of ⅜˝-wide grosgrain ribbon
- Coordinating thread, 12-weight for embroidery and 50-weight for project construction

instructions

All seams are ½˝ unless otherwise noted.

Template pattern is on page 127.

1. Cut the linen, backing fabric, and fusible fleece into rectangles 37˝ × 46˝.

2. Trace the baby sprout template lengthwise in parallel rows on the paper side of the fusible web 84 times—80 for the green fabrics and 4 for the linen fabric.

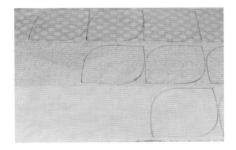

3. Align the green print fabric strips over the rows on the adhesive side of the fusible web. Press.

4. Cut the shapes out along the traced lines.

5. Leaving a ½˝ seam allowance along all 4 edges of the linen fabric, remove the paper backing and fuse the shapes to the linen fabric, 8 across and 10 down, as shown in the diagram. Butt the edges of the appliqué.

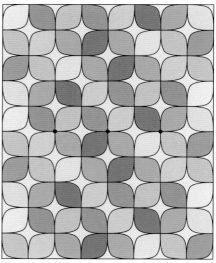

Carrier cover diagram

6. Machine appliqué the shapes to the linen using your favorite stitch type. I used a straight stitch ⅛˝ from the edge of each appliqué.

7. Press the 4 linen appliqué pieces onto the backing fabric 1″ in from the raw edge on the bottom left-hand corner.

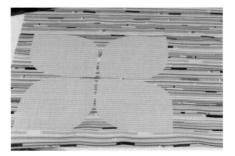

8. Hand stitch around each linen appliqué piece using a 12-weight thread.

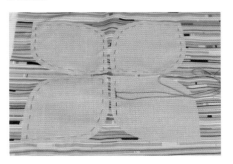

9. Press the fusible fleece to the wrong side of the backing fabric. Place the backing and front pieces right sides together. Stitch ½″ from the edge around all 4 sides, leaving a 4″–6″ opening for turning.

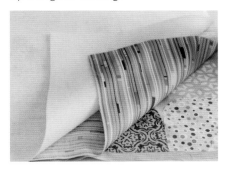

10. Clip the corners and turn right side out and topstitch ⅛″ from the edge on all 4 sides, closing the opening.

11. Cut 3 pieces of ribbon, each 21″ long. Stitch the center of each ribbon to the center of each of the sprouts along the center of the carrier, located as shown on the diagram (page 124).

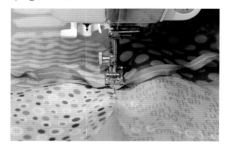

12. Tie the carrier quilt onto the carrier handle.

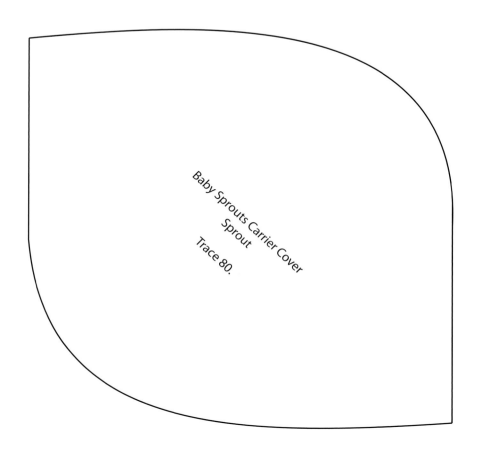

Baby Sprouts Carrier Cover
Sprout
Trace 80.

hild up with this
nspired towel after
imming.

BY

18 hooded panda towel

Finished towel: *fits toddlers to young children*

MATERIALS

- 1 black bath towel
- 1 white bath towel
- 1 white hand towel
- White chalk

> **✳ note**
>
> *The black and white bath towels should be identical in size.*

instructions

Template pattern is on pullout page P1.

1. Fold the black towel in half, matching the shorter ends together. Place the panda back template on the towel, aligning the edges of the template with the edges of the towel. Use a piece of chalk to trace around the template. Then use a rotary ruler and cutter and extend the 5″ strip past the template to the fold of the towel. Finish cutting out along the chalk lines.

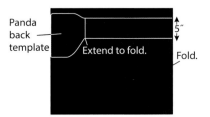

2. Lay the panda back cutout toward the top of the white towel. Pin in place, but don't pin the outside edges of the towels together yet.

3. Trace the panda paw template on the black towel with the piece of white chalk. Cut out 1 paw. Repeat and cut out 3 more paws.

4. Stitch 2 paw pieces together with a ½˝ seam allowance and zigzag stitch to secure the raw edge or serge the curved edge. Leave the straight side open for turning. Turn the paw right side out. Repeat this step to make 1 more complete unit.

5. Insert the raw edges of the paws between the black and white layers of the towel appliqué at both ends of the towels. Pin in place. Stitch the panda back appliqué onto the white towel using a zigzag stitch, securing the paws in place on the towel ends.

6. Center the long side of the hand towel on the top of the white towel. Pin and stitch this long side in place.

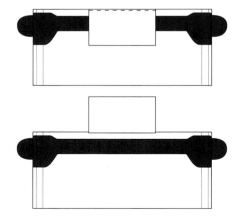

7. Fold the towel in half, with right sides together, matching up the paws and hand towel edges. Stitch across the top of the hand towel to the fold to create the hood.

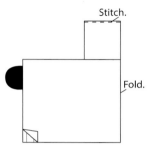

8. Cut 3 squares 5″ × 5″ from the black towel scraps.

9. Fold a square diagonally in half and then in half again (perpendicular to the first fold), creating a prairie point. All the raw edges should be along one side. Stitch the raw-edge side in place. Repeat this step for the other 2 black squares.

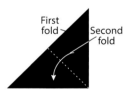

10. Hand stitch 2 of the prairie points to the hood of the towel for the panda's ears. Stitch the third prairie point to the back of the towel for the panda's tail.

Babies up to nine months old will comfortably cuddle up in this little sleep sack for some sweet dreams.

19 sleep baby bunting

MATERIALS

- 1 yard of white fleece
- ¾ yard of knit fabric
- 20″ zipper
- Snap kit

instructions

All seams are ½″ unless otherwise noted.

Template patterns are on pullout page P1 and page 140.

1. Cut out the sleeper pieces from the fleece.

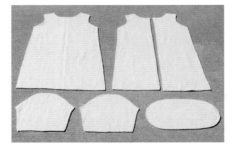

2. Match the zipper and the sleeper center front with right sides facing. Pin and stitch in place. Zigzag or serge the raw edge. Repeat this step for the opposite side of the sleeper front. Topstitch the seams.

3. Check that the zipper is completely closed. Place the sleeper front and back pieces right sides together. Pin and stitch the shoulder seams. Zigzag or serge the raw edges.

Figure B

Figure C

4. Pin the top curved edge of the sleeve to the sleeve opening on the sleeper front and back pieces (Figure A). Stitch in place. Zigzag or serge the raw edges (Figures B and C). Repeat this step for the second sleeve.

Figure A

5. Cut 2 pieces of knit fabric 3″ × 6½″. Fold each in half lengthwise, with wrong sides together. With right sides facing, pin and stitch the raw sides together for each sleeve cuff. Zigzag or serge the raw edges. Turn the seam toward the fleece and topstitch in place.

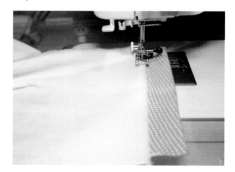

6. Match the sides and underarm seams of the front and back of the sleeper, with right sides facing. Pin and stitch continuously from the bottom of the sleeper to the bottom of the knit cuff. Repeat on the other side. Zigzag or serge the raw edges.

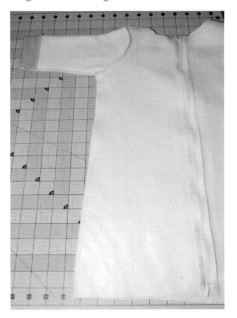

7. Cut a piece of knit fabric 2″ × 13″ on the bias. Fold the strip in half lengthwise, with wrong sides together, and press. Fold the right top corner down to the long raw edge so that the raw edges match up. Repeat for the left side of the strip.

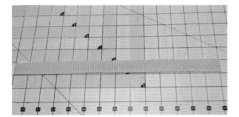

8. Pin the raw edges of the strip to the right side of the sleeper neck, with right sides together. Stitch the collar in place and zigzag or serge the raw edge to finish. Topstitch the raw edge to the wrong side of the sleeper neck.

9. With right sides together, pin the bottom piece all around to the foot of the sleeper. Stitch in place and zigzag or serge the raw edge.

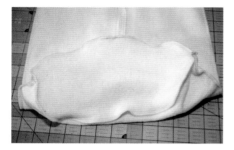

10. Trace the *sleep.* letters onto the paper side of the fusible web and cut them out. Press the adhesive side of the fusible web to the wrong side of the knit fabric. Cut out the letters, remove the paper backing, and press the letters in place on the front of the sleeper. Machine appliqué the letters using your favorite stitch type.

11. Cut out 2 sleeper snap tabs from the knit fabric. With right sides together, stitch around the outside edges. Leave the straight side open for turning. Turn the tab right side out and place the raw edge along the left side of the zipper on the top-stitched seam just below the collar. The purpose of the tab is to cover the zipper pull so it does not poke the baby's neck, so make sure the tab will cover the pull completely. Stitch with a ⅛˝ seam to tack the tab in place.

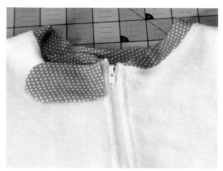

12. Fold the tab back over the raw edge and topstitch with a ¼˝ seam to hide the raw edge of the tab. Follow the manufacturer's instructions and attach a snap to the round end of the tab.

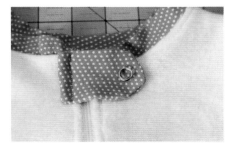

13. Attach the other part of the snap to the sleeper on the right-hand side. The placement of the snap on the tab will determine the corresponding placement of the snap on the front of the sleeper. Before you stitch, add a small piece of fleece to the wrong side to stabilize the snap.

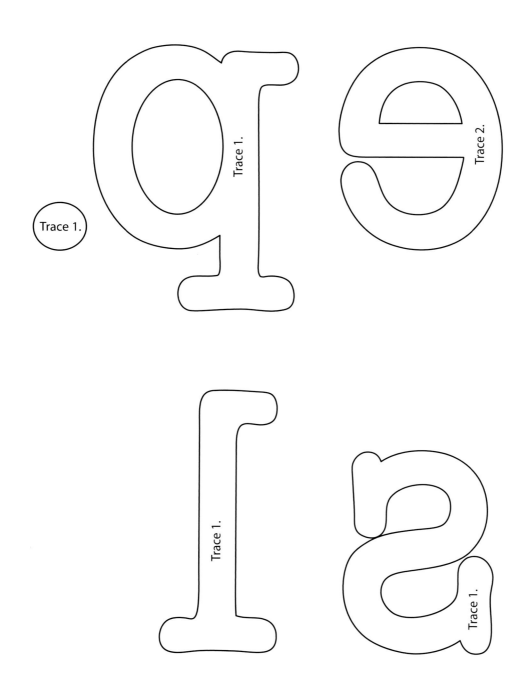

Trace 1.

Trace 1.

Trace 2.

Trace 1.

Trace 1.

resources

FABRICS

Using quality fabrics is key to having a long-lasting quilt or project that you can cherish for many years. The following is a list of manufacturers whose fabrics were used and featured in this book.

- Alexander Henry Fabrics
- Clothworks
- Free Spirit Fabrics
- Henry Glass Fabrics
- Michael Miller Fabrics
- Moda Fabrics
- Riley Blake Designs
- Robert Kaufman Fabrics
- Timeless Treasures Fabrics
- Ty Pennington Fabrics
- Westminster Fibers

SEWING MACHINES

Having the right sewing machine can make a world of difference. Janome (janome.com) is one of the leading machine manufacturers in the industry and provides innovative solutions to make the sewing experience that much more enjoyable. The following are the Janome machines I used to create all these fun and exciting projects.

- Janome Memory Craft 6500P
- Janome Serger 1100D
- Janome CoverPro 1000CPX

NOTIONS

Notions are like the food staples in baking, but for sewing. Threads, scissors, needles, and more are essential for creating any kind of project with fabrics. The following are notion manufacturers whose products are featured in this book and can be found at your local fabric and quilt store.

- American & Efird
- American Felt and Craft
- Aurifil Threads
- C&T Publishing
- Classic Crystal by Lee
- Fairfield Processing
- Fiskars/Gingher
- Luna Quilt Batting by Moda
- Mary Ellen's Best Press
- Pellon
- Prym Consumer USA
- Quiltsmart
- Sewline
- ByAnnie's Soft and Stable

As a young girl, Angela Yosten was influenced by many talented people. While her mother taught her how to sew and encouraged all things arts and crafts–related, her father taught her how to be independent and figure things out on her own. Her grandmothers and great-grandmother also influenced her with their special talents of knitting, sewing, and art. She has always enjoyed drawing, painting, and designing, but it was not until she had her own children that she was inspired to find her way back into the sewing room and discover her own style.

When she is not working as a web developer, she can most likely be found in her sewing room. She finds it thrilling when she can design something new for one of her children or decor for her home. She is often intrigued by everyday items and loves to explore different ways to translate them to fabric. Many of her designs and tutorials can be found on her website (angelayosten.com).

Most of all, she enjoys spending time with her family and cherishing every little moment life has to offer. She feels very fortunate to have such a wonderful husband and amazing children who support her obsession to design and who encourage her in everything that she aspires to do.

Angela is the author of *Stop. Go. Quilt. Sew!* and a contributor to *Modern Blocks*, *Fresh Fabric Treats*, and *Sweet Celebrations with the Moda Bake Shop Chefs*.

Also by Angela Yosten:

Also featuring Angela Yosten:

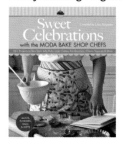

stashBOOKS

fabric arts for a handmade lifestyle

If you're craving beautiful authenticity in a time of mass-production...Stash Books is for you. Stash Books is a line of how-to books celebrating fabric arts for a handmade lifestyle. Backed by C&T Publishing's solid reputation for quality, Stash Books will inspire you with contemporary designs, clear and simple instructions, and engaging photography.

www.stashbooks.com

Ollie the Owl
Feathers

Cut 2 for
each feather.

Ollie the Owl
Feet

Cut 4.

Leave 3" opening for turning and
stuffing on one side.

Leave 2″–3″ o
turning an

Animal
Bo

Cut 2 for e
1 from linen
1 from pri

Sleep Baby Bunting

Snap Tab

Cut 2 from knit fabric.

Sleep Baby Bunting
Front and Back

Cut 2 from fleece.

Cut 1 on fold from fleece for back.

pening for
stuffing.

Rattles
dy

ach turtle:
for belly and
t for back.